TO INHERIT THE SKIES

FROM SPITFIRE TO TORNADO

BRITAIN'S AIR DEFENCE TODAY

TO INHERIT THE SKIES

FROM SPITFIRE TO TORNADO

BRITAIN'S AIR DEFENCE TODAY

Air Vice Marshal R A Mason CB CBE MA RAF

BRASSEY'S (UK)
(a member of the Maxwell Macmillan Pergamon Publishing Group)

LONDON · OXFORD · WASHINGTON · NEW YORK
BEIJING · FRANKFURT · SAO PAULO · SYDNEY · TOKYO · TORONTO

First edition 1990.

UK editorial offices: Brassey's, 50 Fetter Lane, London EC4A 1AA
orders: Brassey's, Headington Hill Hall, Oxford OX3 0BW

USA editorial offices: Brassey's, 8000 Westpark Drive, First Floor,
McLean, Virginia 22102
orders: Macmillan, Front and Brown Streets, Riverside,
New Jersey 08075

Library of Congress Cataloging-in-Publication Data
Mason, R. A.
     To inherit the skies: from Spitfire to Tornado: Britain's air
defence today/R. A. Mason.—1st ed.
   1. Great Britain—Air Defenses.   Military—History.   2 Great
Britain. Royal Air Force—History.   I. Title.
   UG735.07M37   1990   358.4'145'0941—dc20   90–38537

British Library Cataloguing in Publication Data
Mason, R. A.
   To inherit the skies: from Spitfire to Tornado:
   Britain's air defence today
   I. Title
   358.400941

     ISBN 0–08–040708–0 (Hardcover).

Printed in Great Britain by BPCC Wheatons Ltd, Exeter

Dedication

The book commemorates the
ultimate sacrifice of those who secured
the skies over Britain in 1940 and is
dedicated to the men and women of
the Royal Air Force who are today the
worthy inheritors of that legacy.

Acknowledgements

The author is extremely grateful for the wholehearted cooperation in compiling this account which he received from Royal Air Force aircrew, groundcrew and staffs. He drew heavily on Francis K Mason's excellent study, *Battle over Britain* for much of the detailed combat reference. The author is, however, solely responsible for the accuracy or otherwise of facts and their interpretation, without any endorsement by the Royal Air Force or any other agency of the United Kingdom Government. The author wishes to acknowledge the substantial assistance in research which he received from Mr Chris Hobson, Head Librarian at the RAF Staff College, and from Mrs Jean Hollis in the preparation of the manuscript. Crown copyright photographs are reproduced with the permission of the Controller HMSO. Finally, he wishes to thank all the photographers who have generously contributed their photographs.

Glossary

AA	Anti-aircraft
AAR	Air-to-air refuelling
Ab Initio	Inexperienced aircrew on first operational tour of duty
AEO	Air Electronics Officer
AE op	Air Electronics Operator
AEW	Airborne Early Warning
AFB	Air Force Base
AI	Air Interception
AIM	Air Intercept Missile
AOC	Air Officer Commanding
AO C-in-C	Air Officer Commanding-in-Chief
AVM	Air Vice Marshal
AWACS	Airborne Warning and Control Systems
Barrier	Patrol line flown by Shackletons of No 8 Squadron
Bear	NATO codename for Soviet Tupolev 95 long range bomber or maritime reconnaissance aircraft
Bogey	Aircrew slang for hostile aircraft
CAP	Combat Air Patrol
CH	Chain Home radar station
CRC	Control and Reporting Centre
CRP	Control and Reporting Post
CTTO	Central Trials and Tactics Organisation
CW	Continuous Wave
ECCM	Electronic Counter Counter Measures
ECM	Electronic Counter Measures
EW	Electronic Warfare
EWO	Electronic Warfare Officer
FGA	Fighter Ground Attack
GCI	Ground Controlled Interception
Fourship	Aircrew slang for a formation of four aircraft
'G' loading	Measurement of gravitational pressure by aircraft manoeuvre
HAS	Hardened Aircraft Shelter
IDRO	Identification and reporting officer
IFF	Identification Friend or Foe
MC	Master Controller
MET	Meteorology or weather forecast
MINIVAL	Locally organised simulated wartime uinit exercise
NBC	Nuclear, Biological and Chemical protection
OCU	Operational Conversion Unit
OEU	Operational Evaluation Unit
OTU	Operational Training Unit
PD	Pulse Doppler
PI	Practice Interception
QFI	Qualified Flying Instructor
QRA	Quick Readiness Alert
QWI	Qualified Weapons Instructor
Retread	Experienced aircrew converting to another aircraft
R/T	Radio Telephone
SAM	Surface-to-air missile
Six O'clock	Aircrew slang for area immediately behind one's aircraft
Skyflash	Radar guided air-to-air missile
SOC	Sector Operations Centre
SOP	Standard Operating Procedure
Staffel	Flight of German fighters
STO	Squadron Training Officer
Schwarm	Pair of German fighters
TACEVAL	NATO standardised unit exercise simulating wartime conditions
TACO	Tactical Air Director
TWU	Tactical Weapons Unit
UKADGE	United Kingdom Air Defence Ground Environment
UKADR	United Kingdom Air Defence Region
WOC	War Operations Centre

Foreword

Chief of the Air Staff
Air Chief Marshal Sir Peter Harding GCB ADC FRAeS CBIM RAF

Fifty years ago the Royal Air Force was at the forefront of what we now recognise as the greatest air battle of this century and one of the most decisive events of the Second World War. Victory in the Battle of Britain was essential for the survival of Great Britain and the eventual liberation of Western Europe, and that victory depended on our air defences.

Now, as in 1940, the air defence of the United Kingdom remains one of the principal tasks of the Royal Air Force. As Tony Mason outlines in this book, Royal Air Force equipment has changed a great deal in 50 years but the spirit, dedication and skills of our people have not. The Royal Air Force of today still relies upon well trained, highly motivated and courageous men and women in order to fulfil its operational commitments. And not only in the cockpit – it is important to remember that an effective Air Force depends as much on the ground crew, who keep the station in working order and the aircraft serviceable as on the abilities of the aircrew that operate them.

The famous stations and the famous squadrons mentioned in this book are very much part of our heritage. We cannot afford to ignore their history, and the lessons we learnt 50 years ago are still being applied. I have every confidence that our stations, our squadrons and our modern air defenders are worthy 'inheritors of the skies!'

Peter Harding

Contents

Acknowledgements
Glossary
Foreword

Chapter One

THE OPERATIONAL ENVIRONMENT

I N EARLY JUNE 1940 General Edward Milch, Inspector General of the Luftwaffe flew low over the beaches of Dunkirk.

Below him lay the evidence of overwhelming German victory: abandoned and destroyed tanks, guns, vehicles, small arms, ammunition, clothing, military stores, of every kind. Some 300,000 British soldiers had been rescued, but all their heavy armour and artillery had been lost, units were scattered and the British Isles were as defenceless as at any time in their history. At the time, the consequences were taken for granted by friend and enemy alike. Britain would surrender, or negotiate peace terms with Hitler. He had already begun drafting a peace treaty in May.

The Last Line of Defence

But on 18 June, the Prime Minister, Winston Churchill addressed the House of Commons, declaring the country's inflexible resolve to continue the war alone and concluded: 'Let us therefore brace ourselves to our duties, and so bear ourselves that, if the British Empire and its Commonwealth last for a thousand years, men will say "This was their finest hour".'

At first it was regarded as magnificent but unrealistic rhetoric, not least by Hitler. His armies, after all, had overrun Czechoslovakia, Poland, Denmark, Norway, Holland, Belgium, Luxembourg and France. Italy and Austria were allies; his Russian flank had been secured by a non-aggression pact with Stalin; Spain under General Franco appeared inclined to become an ally, while the United States, albeit

sympathetic to the British cause, did not seem disposed to intervene.

By 16 July Hitler was not so sure, and in his War Directive No 16 ordered preparations to begin for an invasion of England.

'As England, despite her hopeless military situation, still shows no sign of willingness to come to terms, I have decided to prepare, and if necessary to carry out, a landing operation against her.'

Two weeks later the focus of his strategy sharpened. War Directive No 17:

'In order to establish the necessary conditions for the final conquest of England I intend to intensify air and sea warfare against the English homeland. I therefore order as follows:
1. The German Air Force is to overpower the English Air Force with all the forces at its command in the shortest possible time. The attacks are to be directed primarily against flying units, their ground installations and their supply organisations but also against the aircraft industry, including that manufacturing anti-aircraft equipment.
2. The intensification of the air war may begin on or after 5 August. The exact time is to be decided by the Air Force after the completion of preparations and in the light of the weather.

The Course of the Battle

It had taken time for the Luftwaffe to move its squadrons from their bases in Germany forward to captured and newly built airfields in France, the Low Countries, Denmark and Norway. Attacks during June and July were consistent but haphazard, hitting convoys in the channel and various targets in the United

Kingdom. But the RAF's Fighter Command had already lost 435 pilots and 453 Spitfires and Hurricanes between 10 May and 20 June in the final stages of the Battle for France.

By 1 July, the Luftwaffe had almost completed its deployment westwards, ultimately reaching a combat strength of 2,800 aircraft, of which approximately 1,100 were fighters, 1,500 were bombers, and 200 reconnaissance. Fighter Command had 591 aircraft combat ready and 1,200 pilots available. These figures however concealed shortages of groundcrew, spares and equipment and the fact that at this stage it was not uncommon for a fighter pilot to join combat with a total of 15 flying hours.

The 'official' date for the beginning of the Battle of Britain is 10 July, but in the previous few days 18 fighters and 13 pilots had been lost in engaging over a dozen raids, each comprising over 50 aircraft. Indeed, No 54 Squadron's diary for 10 July recorded, 'As a result of the first phase of the Battle of Britain, the Squadron could only muster 8 aircraft and 13 pilots.' On the 10th, over 130 German fighters were involved in attacks on a convoy in the Channel and on mainland targets in the west of England and Wales. Later in the month, the scale of attacks increased, but numerical losses on each side remained comparatively light. Of greater concern to Fighter Command's Commander-in-Chief, Sir Hugh Dowding, was the fact that, in human terms, they included more than 80 squadron and flight commanders. These key men were inevitably replaced by pilots with very little experience, if any, of leading formations into combat.

On 12 August, the Luftwaffe began its concentrated campaign against the RAF with raids against the main radar early warning stations on the south coast: Dover, Rye, Pevensey, and Ventnor, together with heavy attacks on Manston and Hawkinge airfields.

Bridging the generation gap. Spitfire P7350, late of No 266 Squadron with Tornado F3 2E908 of No 5 Squadron over the F3s of No 229 OCU at Coningsby *(Sgt Rick Brewell)*

Thereafter the weight of Luftwaffe attacks was concentrated on RAF bases and the aircraft factories supporting them. On 15 August the Luftwaffe flew 1,786 sorties, on the 16th over 1,700, on the 18th 1,000, on 24 August over 1,000 and between then and 6 September 10,000 more. Sir Hugh Dowding first rotated squadrons between the 'front line' 11 Group and those further west and north, and then extracted experienced pilots from the 'resting' squadrons to fill gaps in the south eastern squadrons. In the 13 days from 24 August, Fighter Command lost 231 pilots including a further serious proportion of squadron and flight commanders. Losses were sustained not just from the guns of the Messerschmitt (ME)109 and 110 fighters, but from the mutually supporting, close formation bomber squadrons. The attackers enjoyed a numerical superiority overall of 3 to 1 and locally often as much as 60 to 1.

Then, on Saturday 7 September the Luftwaffe switched its attack, on the personal direction of Herman Goering, to the City of London. The precise reasons for the change remain uncertain. It seems to have been a combination of factors: a belief that Fighter Command could be annihilated in a final battle to defend the capital city; an underestimation by German intelligence of the residual strength of the RAF; and a desire for revenge fuelled by badly hurt pride after RAF attacks on Berlin during the previous week. Goering himself visited his squadrons in northern France that week and watched them launch their attacks on the Saturday.

RAF radar stations observed an unprecedented concentration of aircraft massing over the Pas de Calais, before an armada of 348 bombers and 617 fighters headed almost due north across the Channel. No diversionary raids took place of the kind which had been successful during the previous three weeks. The whole weight of the attack was suffered by the citizens of London and its suburbs: 448 killed and nearly 1,500 injured. Similar attacks took place on the 9th, 11th and 14th of September.

The Decisive Sunday

On Sunday 15 September, the Battle reached its climax. A cloudless day began quietly with isolated Luftwaffe reconnaissance flights. The first bomber build up was detected by British radars in mid morning when the first waves of a days total of 328 German bomber sorties and 769 fighter escort began their track across the south-east coast towards London. They were attacked by increasingly large numbers of Spitfires and Hurricanes until shortly before noon more than 160 fighters from nine squadrons simultaneously struck 100 Dornier 17 bombers, scattering them across south-east London and making protection by their escorting ME109s virtually impossible. Despite this disaster, a second Luftwaffe wave of 150 Dorniers and Heinkels escorted by further ME109s headed towards London soon after 2 o'clock in the afternoon. They were met first over Kent by 170 Spitfires and Hurricanes; then over east London by Squadron Leader Douglas Bader's five squadron Duxford Wing from 12 Group, and finally by 8 more fighter squadrons from 10 and 11 Groups: a total defensive riposte by nearly 300 fighters.

During the day, Winston Churchill visited Air Vice Marshal Park's Operations Centre in Uxbridge and he watched the plotting markers being pushed across the table as the German squadrons moved towards London. He asked the AOC of 11 Group how many reserves he had left to commit to the battle. 'There are none, Prime Minister', came the historic reply.

Further sporadic attacks along the south and south-west coasts were made during the evening but compared to the major events of the day, they were of little consequence. In the excitement and confusion of the battle, claims were made for the destruction of 185 enemy aircraft. The real total of 76 was more than enough for a devastated Luftwaffe which had been assured by its intelligence staff that Fighter Command had been reduced to a handful of serviceable aircraft and demoralised aircrews. By nightfall on that Sunday evening, thankfully, no reserves had been required. The Battle was won. Battle of Britain Sunday passed into the national calendar of remembrance and thanksgiving. There were to be other days of intense conflict: on 30 September for example over 700 sorties were flown against London, Liverpool and other industrial targets losing 59 aircraft in the process in exchange for 36 RAF fighters. But Luftwaffe losses were

Spitfire refuelling at a
forward airfield September 1940
Below: Ground refuelling in 1990 by Cpl Paul Pollard and SAC Paul Wood *(Cpl G Iverson ABiPP RAF Chivenor)*

becoming increasingly serious; the JU88, hitherto the least vulnerable attacker, lost 40 aircraft and 160 aircrew from one squadron alone. An order forbade the flight of more than one officer in any one aircraft.

Meanwhile by prodigious efforts and despite the earlier effects of the Luftwaffe, British fighter •production continued to gather momentum. The switching of targets and tactics by the Luftwaffe had brought welcome relief to the Hurricane and Spitfire pilots. On the morning of 16 September there were 160 Spitfires and Hurricanes immediately available as reinforcements with a further 400 accessible within a week. Pilot losses were still heavy, especially when novices tangled with free-hunting swarms of ME109s rather than cutting out the bomber streams. But since 7 September there had been opportunities to give new pilots a familiarisation training flight, perhaps to use a reflector gunsight for the first time. New arrivals might have been able to accrue 20 hours on Spitfires or Hurricanes as the training organisation itself began to benefit from increased aircraft and associated equipment.

As London and other cities began to endure the agonies of the Blitz, through the long winter of 1940–41, and as rumours of invasion intermittently reoccurred, it was not readily apparent in Britain that a great victory had been won. Darkness and moonlight were to remain allies of the German bomber squadrons until the combination of Beaufighter night fighters and airborne radar exacted too heavy a toll in that environment also. But unknown to the British government at the time, Hitler had on 17 September postponed indefinitely his invasion plans and his ambitions were turning more and more towards the east. The Luftwaffe had failed to 'establish the necessary conditions for the final conquest of England'. Its failure had become apparent even to the most stubborn members of the Luftwaffe High Command as they assessed their losses of the second week of September, and especially the impact of Fighter Command's savaging of the raids of Sunday the 15th. Dark days were to remain; British military disasters on land and at sea were still to be faced, but never again would the United Kingdom be threatened by invasion and subjugation by the Wehrmacht. The country would survive to become the spring-

board for the invasion of western Europe and the overthrow of Hitler. Between 10 July and 31 October, Fighter Command lost 915 aircraft, but Luftwaffe losses totalled 1,733. Over 550 British and allied aircrews died, together with unnumbered airmen and airwomen on the ground, many others who contributed in Bomber and Coastal Command squadrons and those who died in flying accidents before they could even reach the front line squadrons. Compared to the total numbers lost by both sides in World War II they were not very many; but in quality, they were incomparable.

Fifty Years On

The direct descendants of Fighter Command in 1940 are now to be found in the men and women, spearheaded by the squadron aircrew, of No 11 Group. Its Headquarters are still at Bentley Priory near Stanmore in Middlesex. Now, however, the Air Officer Commanding's peacetime location is in a modern functional office block a hundred yards away from the elegant room in the Priory where Sir Hugh Dowding commanded his squadrons and fretted, as he had done as a squadron commander in World War I, at the price paid by young men who would never celebrate their victory.

Much has changed in 50 years. Of the bases whose names were familiar to every 10 year old in 1940, some, like Kenley, Debden, Croydon, Kirton in Lindsey, Horchurch, North Weald, Hawkinge, Tangmere, and Duxford either lie peacefully under the plough, or are submerged under housing estates, or provide facilities for civilian aviation, or are preserved in a museum time warp. Others, like Biggin Hill, Manston, Northolt, Digby, Wittering, Church Fenton, Catterick, Turnhouse, Boscombe Down, and Coltishall are still RAF stations but no longer bear responsibilities for air defence. Just one airfield, then a grass-strip in the Catterick Sector of 13 Group which was home for the Blenheims of No 219 Squadron in September 1940 is now, as RAF Leeming, a main fighter operating base.

The Strategic Environment
Now, the whole scene is new. New technology has affected the development of aircraft, weapons, communications and almost all sup-

porting equipment. But many basic procedures
and their associated skills still remain. Above
all, as the following chapters will illustrate, the
men and women serving in the modern Royal
Air Force are worthy inheritors of their predecessors of 1940.

It is in the overall strategic environment that
the most obvious change can be seen and
indeed many other differences between 1990
and 1940 flow from it.

In 1940 Fighter Command was not well
prepared for the Battle of Britain, despite
strenuous efforts by specific individuals, especially Air Marshal Dowding, over the previous
few years. Before the development of radio
direction-finding by pioneers such as Robert
Watson-Watt it had been widely believed that
attacking aircraft would not be located in time
for fighter aircraft to take off, climb to height
and intercept them before they reached their
targets. Until the development of monoplane
fighters such as the Spitfire, Hurricane and
Messerschmitt 109, there had been little
difference between the speed of bombers and
fighters, and even with early warning the older
biplanes could present little threat to bombers
already at their operating height of 15–20,000
feet. Thankfully, the Hurricane was in squadron service in 1940, the Spitfire was gradually
joining it, and 51 Chain Home Radio
Direction-Finding installations were in position, supplemented by several mobile units to
fill gaps and stand in for damaged permanent
sites.

Before 1939, war with Germany had
become an increasing probability, but no-one
had forseen the speed and comprehensive
success of Blitzkreig, culminating in the catas-
trophic collapse of France in June 1940 which
left Britain completely alone against an enemy
who controlled the European coastline from
Bordeaux to the North Cape of Norway and
the airfields immediately behind it. There was
no defence in depth, and the nearest German
airfields in the Pas de Calais were only 40 miles
from the south coast, or seven minutes flying
time for a Messerschmitt 109. The situation in
1990 is very different.

If 1940 in Britain was a year for desperate,
determined struggle for survival which, even if
successful, would lead to a dark uncertain
future, 1990 is perhaps the greatest year of

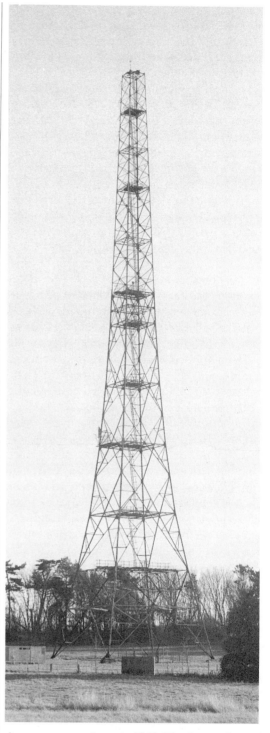

A monument to victory in 1940. The frame of one of
the original Chain Home transmitter masts at RAF
Bawdsey. The invention and application of radio
direction finding made a critical contribution to the
Battle of Britain. Without it, timely interception
would have been impossible *(RAF Wattisham/Crown
Copyright)*

hope for permanent peace in Europe since the end of the Second World War. As eastern Europe and the Soviet Union seek to replace totalitarian regimes with open societies and establish the freedoms which the United Kingdom has taken for granted for centuries, there is hope that a more recent military threat to Britain will recede. However, until political stability is achieved by those countries now pursuing reform, and until large reductions in their armed forces are implemented, Britain's current defensive posture must remain.

The air threat to the United Kingdom in 1940 originated on airfields a mere few score miles away; it could now be mounted from bases in different continents and, thanks to modern weapon technology, lay waste a greater area with many fewer aircraft than those which pierced our defences in September 1940. Provision for the safety of the homeland by a secure air defence will remain a responsibility of government long after the current divisions between East and West have dissolved.

The first and most important difference in the strategic environment for United Kingdom air defence between 1990 and 1940 is that now Britain is a member of the closely coordinated North Atlantic Treaty Organisation, with 16 independent nations committed, within the terms of Article 51 of the United Nations Charter, to mutual defence. Indeed, the security of the United Kingdom is of considerable importance not just to British citizens but to allies who, in the event of war, would come to depend on these islands as a vital link between the European theatre and the United States and Canada. The deterrent posture maintained by NATO for over 40 years rests on both residual nuclear capability and, in the strategy of flexible response, the preservation of defensive options which start with the defence of allied territory right up to the borders with Warsaw Pact countries. That strategy will support those responsibilities until large scale force reductions are achieved and a practical cooperative security agreement with the Soviet Union and her allies has been reached. That is the context for the examination of the activities of 11 Group and supporting units in 1990.

At present, NATO continues to face numerically superior in-position Warsaw Pact air and ground forces. In the event of conflict breaking out in Europe, happily now increasingly less threatening, the Alliance would be dependent on heavy reinforcements flowing into Europe by air and sea from North America. The integrity of United Kingdom air space, and the availability of airfields, harbours and associated installations, would be essential to ensure that such reinforcements could take place. Indeed, if current arms reduction negotiations in Vienna are successful, the ability to reinforce in a crisis may become even more important because of the relative proximity of the Soviet Union to central Europe compared to the distance across the Atlantic separating the United States and Canada from the rest of the Western Alliance. In addition, the United Kingdom provides much needed defence in depth to operations on the European mainland and is the location of several squadrons of RAF Tornado GR1 and United States Air Force (USAF) F111 strike aircraft which would contribute directly to the counter-air and air land battles. In sum, air defence of the United Kingdom is now within an alliance framework and not an isolated, purely national concern. Therefore a simple comparison of the size of Fighter Command in 1940 and that of 11 Group in 1990 could give a very misleading impression of the extent of air defence provision to these islands.

Changes In Scale
On 15 September 1940, the Fighter Command Order of Battle listed 68 squadrons within four Groups. The Headquarters of No 10 were at Rudloe Manor, near Bath in Wiltshire and coordinated protection over the west and south-west of England. 13 Group protected the northern flank from Ouston, near Newcastle, with squadrons as far afield as Wick and Sumburgh in the Shetlands. No 12 Group, located at Hucknall near Nottingham, and commanded by Air Vice Marshal Trafford Leigh-Mallory, provided the air defence of northern East Anglia and the Midlands. The front line of south-east England was protected by the squadrons of Air Vice Marshal Keith Park's 11 Group at its well known headquarters at Uxbridge. In 1990, Air Vice Marshal Bill Wratten, Air Officer Commanding 11 Group, is responsible to the Air Officer

Commander-in-Chief Strike Command for the air defences of all four regions.

Air Vice Marshal Wratten's responsibilities as AOC 11 Group are very extensive and, in two important aspects, exceed those discharged by Sir Hugh Dowding in 1940. He is tasked to ensure that all 11 Group forces, in the air and on the ground, are fully trained and ready to meet the demands implicit and explicit in national contingency plans and NATO strategy. In practice that still means coming to war readiness in hours rather than days.

11 Group must be fully prepared. In 1940, after the fall of France, Sir Hugh Dowding had a critically important few weeks in which to prepare his squadrons for a major battle and accelerate the flow of new pilots into the front line. In a conflict under current circumstances in Europe the air battle would be fought by the crews already on the front line squadrons, supplemented by others on the Tactical Weapons Units, the Operational Conversion Units and those still current in their flying status but employed on staff and other ground duties. This demand for a constant operational preparedness must be tested regularly in conditions which are as close to those of war time as possible.

The AOC's 'territory' is the United Kingdom Air Defence Region (UKADR) which extends from the British Isles northwards beyond the Faeroe Islands, north-eastwards to the boundary with Norwegian and Danish regions, then east, south-east and south along boundaries with West German, Dutch, Belgian and French areas of defensive responsibility. In 1940, there was no threat from the west or north, but now several Soviet aircraft have the range to attack the United Kingdom from the direction of the Atlantic, and so the Air Defence Region stretches out into the western Atlantic, excluding, of course, the airspace of the neutral Republic of Eire. As a result, AOC 11 Group is responsible on behalf of CINCUKAIR for the efficient manning of the radar units which ensure early warning of air attack to the UKADR and for its policing. The region extends for over 1,000 nautical miles from north to south and encompasses half a million square miles of airspace. Just as the squadrons of 10 and 11 Groups provided protection for Channel convoys in 1940, so

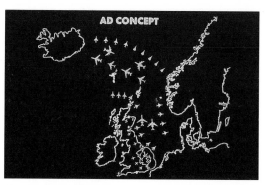

Air Defence Concept of Operations: Tornadoes and Phantoms deployed out over the North Atlantic and North Sea: behind them the AEW and AAR aircraft; Hawks close to the UK and behind them the surface-to-air defences

today, AVM Wratten's tasks include the provision of air defence of maritime forces operating within the region. One significant responsibility which 11 Group now has, which Sir Hugh Dowding did not enjoy, is for all Tactical Weapons Unit and Operational Conversion Unit flying training and for Fighter Control personnel training. As a result there can be complete coordination of operational training from the 'ab initio' officer right through to final Combat Readiness. Technology has added further responsibility to today's commander. The descendants of the 1940 Chain Home Radio Direction-Finding installations are the Ground Radar Units of No 11 Group, ringing the coastline from Saxa Vord in the Shetlands to Portreath in the south-west. In addition there is the airborne early warning provided, in its last venerable year, by the Shackletons of No 8 Squadron and by the infinitely more capable Boeing E3D Sentry, due to enter RAF service in late 1990. Flying and ground training for the Shackletons and Sentry crews is also the responsibility of 11 Group.

The Threat

In 1940 there was no ambiguity about the source, extent and potential of the air threat to the British Isles. It came from the Luftwaffe's *Luftflotten* 2, 3 and 5, based in north-east France and the Low Countries, north-west France and Scandinavia respectively. Fortunately for the United Kingdom, it took the Luftwaffe several weeks after the fall of France to establish forward airbases and the necessary logistic support in the newly conquered territories of western Europe. Then, when regular operations did begin, they lacked clear cut coordination towards a specific objective until the issue of Hitler's Directive No 17, identifying the RAF as the primary target. In the meanwhile they attacked convoys, harbour industrial centres and military installations, an approach which, as has been noted above, caused a steady but not critical loss rate to Fighter Command. Only when their attacks were coordinated and concentrated during August and early September did the Luftwaffe come within reach of victory and stretch the fighter crews to their limits.

In a conflict between NATO and the Warsaw Pact, circumstances would be very different until such time as the Soviet Air Force implements the 'Defensive Doctrine' and associated reduction and redeployment of squadrons promised by Soviet leaders. Current Warsaw Pact air doctrine envisages a large scale air attack on western Europe, including the British Isles, with an initial phase lasting 36–48 hours designed, exactly as intended by the Luftwaffe 50 years ago, to deny opposing air forces in Europe any influential role in the subsequent conflict. Not, on this occasion, as a precursor to an invasion of the British Isles, but in preparation for ground force attack across NATO's eastern boundaries. Consequently, the United Kingdom Air Defence would be highly unlikely to face the entire weight of Soviet air attack, but radar installations and airfields would be likely to be targetted by medium and long range bombers from Soviet Frontal Aviation and from the Soviet Air Force's centrally controlled bomber regiments, while harbours and maritime forces would be sought out by aircraft of Soviet Naval Aviation. The air defence of the United Kingdom, would under those circumstances, be coordinated with that of the European allies and the United States; hence the close peacetime cooperation between the units of 11 Group and especially the squadrons of the Norwegian and Danish air forces along the most likely axes of attack from the Baltic and Scandinavian regions, and with USAF units deployed in Iceland.

The bulk of the attacking forces would be likely to comprise TU 16 Badger, TU 22 Blinder, TU 22M Backfire, TU 95 Bear and SU 24 Fencer bombers. Unlike the circumstances of 1940, however, these aircraft would not all need to overfly their targets, as the Soviet Air Forces have been equipped more and more with various kinds of stand-off weapons. It is therefore increasingly important for the fighter squadrons of 11 Group to be able to intercept the attackers well before they reach the British coastline, quite apart from the requirement to protect allied shipping in the north-west Atlantic and North Sea. This need for a forward defence at the extremities of the UKADR explains the nature of 11 Group's peacetime squadron activities and the extremely important contribution of airborne early warning aircraft.

The Defensive Response

While far fewer in number than their predecessors in 1940, the nine fighter squadrons of 11 Group, comprising Tornado F3 and Phantom F4J and F4GR2 aircraft, supplemented by Hawks from the Tactical Weapons Units and Phantoms and Tornadoes from the Operational Conversion Units, have a faster rate of climb, longer endurance, far longer range and heavier armament than the Hurricane and

Soviet Air Force TU16 Badger over the North Sea *(No 101 Squadron/Crown Copyright)*

Spitfire. While still carrying guns, the Tornadoes and Phantoms are also armed with short range heat-seeking Sidewinder missiles and beyond-visual-range guided missiles which, in combat, would not necessarily require visual identification of an enemy. The ability of the Tornadoes and Phantoms to mount long range Combat Air Patrols, and to engage at maximum range, is further enhanced by the availability of in-flight refuelling, provided by Victors, VC 10s and Tristars of No 1 Group.

The actual fighting of the battle would, in many respects, be reminiscent of the situation in 1940. Just as Sir Hugh Dowding switched his squadrons from one area of activity to another, depending on the location and extent of the threat, so the modern Air Defence Commander would deploy his assets according to similar principles. A major difference, however, is that because of their range, and access to in-flight refuelling, Tornadoes and Phantoms would not necessarily need to deploy from their main bases to cover the extremities of the UKADR. The UKADR is divided into two sectors: one covering the southern, the other the northern region. In war, the actual broad allocation of aircraft to incoming raids would be the task of the Sector Commanders. Either could request assistance from the other, with the ultimate responsibility for priorities resting with the Air Defence Commander: CINCUKAIR, who delegates the responsibility to AOC 11 Group. However, just as in 1940 some aircraft were detached from their main bases to operate from forward locations, for example at Wick or Lympne, so some Tornadoes, for example those of Nos 11 and 29 Squadrons, both of which have primary responsibilities for maritime defence, could be deployed to bases which would afford greater concentration over shorter distances from their designated combat areas.

While rapidly advancing technology has, in many ways, facilitated air defence, in one significant respect it has made it more complicated. In 1940 the ability of the ground controller to relay instructions to the fighter pilots was likely to be restricted only by the rudimentary nature of his equipment or by the excited shouts of pilots as they engaged enemy formation. Electronic warfare was in its infancy. General Wolfang Martini, head of the

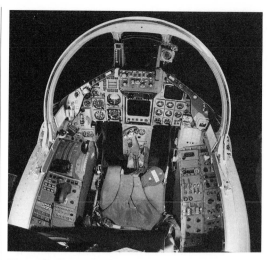

Tornado Front Cockpit *(British Aerospace)*

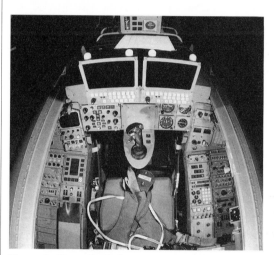

Tornado Rear Cockpit *(British Aerospace)*

Luftwaffe Signals Branch, was fully aware of the critical importance of both the British early warning stations and the ability of fighter controllers to place the Hurricanes and Spitfires in the path of attacking bomber formations, but he had no counter to them other than their physical destruction by direct air attack. In 1990 electronic counter measures (ECM) and defensive counter counter measures (ECCM) are an integral part of air warfare. Just as in 1940, when Dr R V Jones was conducting experiments in jamming the Luftwaffe's bombing navigation systems, the exact details of equipment and techniques remain among the most highly classified of military secrets. Basic laws of physics however, on which they all are based, remain constant.

Radio and radar frequencies can be detected, and once detected, they can be subject to several kinds of interference seeking either to eliminate, distort or 'spoof' them. In 1940, for example, at least one attempt was made by a Czech-speaking German controller, using the call sign 'Apena' one of the Czech squadrons, to cut in on the squadron's voice radio frequency to give a spurious order recalling its aircraft to base.

The Soviet Air Force has large numbers of specialist EW aircraft which could be expected to provide stand-off jamming to the air offensive, while all SAF aircraft carry on board self-protection ECM equipment. As a result, 11 Group fighters, radar installations and fighter controllers regularly rehearse operations in an electronic warfare environment against ECM equipped Canberras of 360 squadron of 1 Group and against EF 111s of the USAF. In 1990 it is not sufficient to be able to fly and fight at night and in all weathers; air defence must continue to be effective when communications between its various components are being degraded by enemy action.

Ground Defences

In 1940 Glenthorn House in the grounds of Bentley Priory was the headquarters of Anti-Aircraft Command, whose General Officer Commanding-in-Chief from 28 July until the end of the war was General Sir Frederick Pile. The relationship between the two Commands could have presented problems because AA Command was an Army organisation, formed the previous year, and General Pile was not subordinate to Air Chief Marshal Dowding. But for obvious purposes aircraft, barrage balloons, searchlights, guns and members of the Observer Corps had to be coordinated in a coherent defensive framework. Happily, the two Commanders-in-Chief established a close personal relationship, cemented by daily meetings in Sir Hugh Dowding's office in the Priory. Even then, however, there were too many – one would have been too many – examples of RAF aircraft being shot down by AA batteries; such incidents are now referred to as 'Blue on Blue'. Sadly, such self inflicted losses also occurred occasionally in the air, throughout the Battle of Britain.

The Royal Observer Corps provided vital information on incoming raids. Here one Observer sights an aircraft, estimating its position and track by reference to the circular chart below the triangle. The second Observer is passing the information to his Group centre by his chestmounted telephone. 15 Sept 1940

In combat through the ages losses have occurred to friendly action, and indeed the individual Standards of the Roman legions and the Colours of British regiments had in common the provision of identity to the units fighting beside them. In the fast moving, often cloud-enshrouded, and increasingly long range combat of the skies, problems of distinguishing between friend and foe are much more difficult. When the modern generation of surface-to-air defences are added to the equation, air forces have another reason for ensuring that as far as possible, ground defences and fighter aircraft are subject to the same highly coordinated command and control.

This is now achieved within 11 Group by placing all anti-aircraft guns and surface-to-air missiles under the direct command of the Air Defence Commander. On behalf of CINCUKAIR, Air Vice Marshal Wratten commands, in addition to his fighter squadron and radar units, squadrons of Bloodhound and Rapier missiles and anti-aircraft guns dispersed throughout the eastern and northern regions of the United Kingdom. The guns and short range Rapiers are operated by men of the RAF Regiment and RAUXAF, the Bloodhounds by men and women of the General Duties Branch.

Continuity and Change

The mantle of responsibility for the integrity of British airspace has now passed from Fighter Command to 11 Group. The basic task remains the same, as do many of the principles which determine the nature of air defence. In 1990 however, the strategic environment, the power and complexity of modern weapons, the advanced technology in modern fighters and the need for constant preparedness determine the way in which the aircrew and groundcrew of 11 Group and supporting units actually train in peacetime. By their visible preparedness they must continue to ensure that no potential enemy will ever make the same miscalculation as Hitler in 1940, who believed that the defeat of the RAF was but a step towards the subjugation of the United Kingdom.

Air Vice Marshal W. J. Wratten
CBE AFC RAF
Air Officer Commanding No 11 Group 1990

Air Vice Marshal Bill Wratten has commanded No 11 Group since March 1989. A graduate of the Royal Air Force College Cranwell, AVM Wratten flew Lightnings and Phantoms before taking command of No 23 Squadron, then equipped with Phantoms in 1975. He commanded RAF Coningsby from 1980 to 1982 before moving to the Falklands to establish and command the base at RAF Stanley.

In common with most senior RAF officers, AVM Wratten's extensive fighter experience has been broadened by tours of duty with different responsibilities. He is a qualified flying instructor, he has flown on both air defence and ground attack squadrons in Germany, he completed a tour of duty as Senior Air Staff Officer at Headquarters No 1 Group, and he has grappled with the task of providing personnel and new weapons for the Service in staff appointments at the Ministry of Defence. He attended the RAF Staff College in 1974 and the Royal College of Defence Studies in 1983. AVM Wratten is therefore well qualified not only to lead the fighter squadrons of his Group, but to place his responsibilities in the overall context of national and Service commitments: attributes which would have been quietly approved by his illustrious predecessor at Bentley Priory in 1940.

Chapter Two

THE MAKING
OF THE FIGHTER
CREW

THE BASIC STATISTICS of the Battle of Britain are straightforward. Despite facing regular odds of 10 to 1 and upwards, the Hurricane and Spitfire pilots destroyed two enemy aircraft for every Royal Air Force fighter lost. In the following chapters not all comparative squadron figures have been given for claims and kills: all are well and honourably recorded in squadron histories and elsewhere. Squadrons were sometimes scrambled early, others a little late; sometimes they met more fighters than bombers, sometimes they fought ME 109s low in fuel, sometimes a *Staffel* fresh to the fray; sometimes they were lucky and sometimes they were not. Sometimes they were fortunate in having flight and squadron commanders who stayed alive long enough to impart their skills to the novices; and sometimes they didn't. If they didn't, the novice lost his major source of combat training.

The biggest single difference, by far, between the fighter crews of 1940 and their descendants in 1990 is the extent and quality of their preparation for combat. Until military disengagement follows the relaxation of political tension, British fighter crews with their NATO colleagues have been prepared in 1990 to respond swiftly to an attack at the outset of a conflict which would be highly unlikely to last more than a few weeks. Supplementary crews with current flying expertise would be culled from staff posts and other areas beyond the front line but there would be no time to expand either recruiting or flying training.

The Battle of Britain was from the outset the stuff of which national legends are born, and Winston Churchill's command of the language in his paean of praise matched the aircrews' command of the skies above England. The odds, the skills, the bravery, the victory would under any circumstances have inscribed history, but when the comparative experience and especially the preparation, or lack of it, of the British crews is examined, the final result is even more incredible. It was a bitter lesson which subsequent generations of RAF leaders have taken to heart: never again would novices be put into battle against hardened veterans.

Pilots

As the British Expeditionary Force struggled home from the Dunkirk disaster, Fighter Command estimated that it needed 500 more pilots to man the front line, sustain training instructor experience levels and absorb casualties. Before the war, it had taken one year to produce a proficient pilot, and two to polish his skills. From 1936 onwards, the inevitability of conflict with Germany became increasingly apparent and successive government plans called for more and more squadrons. In those days, aircraft could be built more quickly than a pilot could be trained and even in the darkest days of early September 1940, there were always reserves of Hurricanes and Spitfires available to replace casualties. In a subsequent despatch, Air Marshal Dowding wrote, 'By the beginning of September the incidence of casualties became so serious that a fresh squadron would become depleted and exhausted before any of the resting and reforming squadrons was ready to take its place. Fighter pilots were no longer being produced in numbers sufficient to fill the gaps in the fighting ranks.'

Pilots were given basic flying training on a mixture of Tiger Moths, Miles Magisters and a handful of newly acquired American Harvards. Basic training of 100 hours was expected to take a year, but by early 1940, 80–90 hours were being flown over 16 weeks. Thereafter, the pilots moved to an 'Operational Training Unit' (OTU) where, in theory, they were converted from pilots who could fly an aeroplane into pilots who could fight in an aeroplane. But despite the increased emphasis on air defence since 1936, there were 31 Bomber OTUs and only three in Fighter Command. Seventy-five per cent of all OTU flying took place on Hawker Hart biplanes. The OTU course was designed with 50–60 hours over six weeks. By July 1940 that was reduced to 10–20 hours solo on Spitfire or Hurricane in 7–14 days with no ground school introduction.

Efforts to expand the training schools were inhibited by shortage of camera guns, reflector sights, armoury and R/T facilities. The vast majority of flying instructors had no operational background and to complicate matters

further the winter of 1939–40 was extremely severe and restricted what little expansion was achieved. Pilots were transferred from Bomber and Coastal Commands, from Army Cooperation and from the Fleet Air Arm. Fifty-eight Royal Navy pilots fought in the Battle; 18 of them were killed. As the Battle intensified, pilots with operational experience were recalled from OTU instructional duties to the front line, reducing the quality of training still further.

The results were inevitable: shorter periods of training, less experienced instructors, less competent arrivals on the front line, higher casualties, increased demands for new pilots, greater pressure on the training establishments . . . a vicious downwards spiral, insoluble as long as the fighter crews were engaged in daily incessant combat. This is why it is impossible to exaggerate the impact of Goering's switch of Luftwaffe attacks to London on 7 September. Londoners paid with their lives for the opportunity given to Fighter Command to regroup and rebuild.

If the aircrew of 11 Group should ever have to fire their guns and missiles in anger again the

Instrument flying instruction in September 1940. The future fighter pilot is under the canopy in the rear seat of the Miles Magister

story would be very different. Numerically there are not many of them, but it is difficult to see how their preparation for combat could be improved. It begins at the Basic Flying Training Schools, progresses through Advanced Flying Training at Valley, Tactical Weapons Instruction at Chivenor and Brawdy and ends at the threshold of the front line at the Operational Conversion Units (OCU) – the successors to the OTUs of 1940 – at Leuchars and Coningsby.

Depending on previous flying experience, perhaps gained as an Air Training Corps Flying Scholar or as a member of a University Air Squadron, the student pilot will complete either 76 or 93 hours on the Jet Provost or the RAFs new Tucano, 75 hours on the Hawk Mk T1 at Valley and a further 52 hours on the Hawk Mk T1A at the Tactical Weapons Unit (TWU). In 1989, the first female pilots began training in the RAF. At present restricted by political decision to non-combat roles, it is unlikely women will graduate to Phantom or Tornado cockpits in the near future.

In July 1987, a number of young men and women arrived at Cranwell to begin the Initial Officers' Training Course, the gate through which all aircrew and ground branch officers enter today's Royal Air Force. As usual, about 80 per cent of them graduated and received their Commission. Most of them moved away to begin preparation for their various responsibilities as junior officers. Ground branch officers dispersed to various specialist schools, navigators went to Finningley and pilots went to Church Fenton or Linton-on-Ouse or simply across the airfield to the flying training squadron at Cranwell. Among the latter was Flight Lieutenant Ian Cook, an ex-Air Training Corps flying scholar, graduate in Computer Science from London University and already holder of a private pilot's licence. In February 1990, he was nearing the half-way point in the combat pilot training course at No 2 Tactical Weapons Unit at Chivenor in North Devon, the last stage of preparation before a front line appointment. He gave the author his personal reflections on the making of a fast jet fighter pilot. Many of his comments readily evoked the very different circumstances of 1940.

When he joined No 3 Flying Training Squadron, subsequently amalgamated with No 1 at Cranwell, he already had 50 civilian flying hours. His first impression of the Jet Provost, flying in low level familiarisation formation over the Lincolnshire countryside, was of the speed of events, even at a relatively moderate 240 knots. He felt 'a long way behind the aircraft'. After learning the need for accuracy in military flying, basic aerobatics and instrument practice he went solo after 13 hours. He recalled specific hurdles which progressively thinned out the course: spinning, night flying, low level navigation and instrument tests. After 100 hours the course was streamed. He, with four others, moved to Group 1, to prepare for single seat fast jet advancement, 11 colleagues entered Group 2 prior to going on to multi-engined, multi-crew selection. Training was closely supervised by individual Qualified Flying Instructors (QFIs) and each young pilot was given two chances to pass the various checkpoints which at the time were regarded as major hurdles and induced a fair amount of psychological pressure. After approximately 12 months, Flight Lieutenant Cook had amassed 151.50 hours on the Jet Provost, had won the best overall flying award and moved across to Valley in North Wales to tackle the next hurdle: the advanced fast jet training course flying the Hawk. Like most young pilots, Flight Lieutenant Cook set his sights on immediate targets rather than long term goals. After six weeks of ground school in which he gained essential theoretical knowledge of the aircraft's systems, emergency procedures and aerodynamic characteristics, he set out on another solo target. He found the general handling conversion phase at 350 knots easier than he had anticipated because of the excellent handling qualities of the Hawk. There was nevertheless a lot to learn in relatively few hours. The greater power and responsiveness of the Hawk allowed much faster transition in sorties between different kinds of exercise. Again, Flight Lieutenant Cook mastered his new environment and, after 84 hours, moved in November 1989 down to No 2 TWU at Chivenor.

There are two Tactical Weapons Units, at Chivenor and Brawdy in West Wales. The objective of the TWU is to introduce pilot and navigator to tactical weapons operations and techniques in order to expand their knowledge

acquired during flying or previous experience
and to qualify the student for fast jet Operational Conversion Unit (OCU) training. The
course lasts for approximately four months,
during which the pilot will accrue a minimum
of 52 log book hours covering all aspects of
RAF fast jet combat flying, including air-to-air
combat, bombing and strafing, tactical formations, air defence and low level evasion. The
instructors are all carefully chosen for their
own proven combat skills, including a number
of QFIs and QWIs (Qualified Weapon
Instructors).

When the student pilot arrives at Brawdy or
Chivenor he is expected to be already a
competent Hawk pilot. He must now learn to
fight. In Flight Lieutenant Cook's quotation
from his instructors: 'Be there and cope!' The
pressure is of a very different kind. Previously
the trainee has been competing with his
contemporaries and against the flying hurdles
placed in front of him. At Chivenor he is
competing against his contemporaries and
against his instructors. He becomes rapidly
and uncomfortably aware of his inexperience.
He must develop the skill, aggression and
determination necessary either to fight his way
to a target and back, or to 'kill' an air-to-air
opponent and survive another day himself. He
is shown combat skills, he must copy them and
make them his own. The gentlemanly encouragement of the flying training environment has
given way to the constructive but hardnosed
'kill or be killed' approach essential for combat
survival. The innocent tail chase of Valley,
where the student sought to keep station on his
gently weaving leader is replaced by the high
'G' turns induced by attempts to place the staff
pilot in his gun sights; turns which will almost
always end with the student sitting squarely in
the instructor's sights at comfortable shooting
distance.

Flight Lieutenant Cook had not studied the
experiences of the Battle of Britain when he
said, 'There is an accumulated pressure build
up in a combat manoeuvring sortie. You always
make mistakes, the staff pilot always seems to
be on your six (i.e. at six o'clock is the pilot's
vernacular for position relative to his own) and
as you return to base you are very tired.' Asked
how he would have liked to have flown three or
four such sorties with real combat every day for

A future fighter pilot climbs aboard the Hawk
simulator at RAF Chivenor *(Cpl G Iverson ABiPP)*

several weeks, without any combat training, he
simply replied, 'You would have been shot
down; a bogey would have been on your tail in
seconds; you need a long time to build up the
skills, quite apart from natural ability and good
luck'. In another comment he explained the
demands of keeping formation at low level,
thinking about the actions of colleagues, anti-
cipating hostile attack and all the while maintaining the objective of the sortie. Not surprisingly, the staff pilots begin with relatively
straightforward combat examples, and then
make them progressively more difficult.

The view of the experienced combat pilot,
typical of the TWU staff, was given by Flight
Lieutenant Jim Gosling of 151 Squadron, a
Jaguar pilot QWI with a total of 2150 hours. In
a tight syllabus, all phases have unique value,
but the five hours allocated to basic combat
manoevring are essential for all fast jet pilots
whether they are going to specialise in offensive operations as in the Tornado GR1, fighter
ground attack as in the Jaguar or Harrier or air
defence interception in the Phantom and
Tornado F3. Flight Lieutenant Gosling
explained how, at the outset of this phase, the
staff pilots manoeuvre reasonably predictably
and then, the better the student responds, the
more aggressive the tuition without destroying
the student's confidence. The implications of
that increase in aggression were obvious in
Flight Lieutenant Gosling's observation that,

Hawks of Nos 63 and 151 Squadron armed with 30mm gun and AIM 9L missiles *(Cpl G Iverson ABiPP)*

Arming a Hawk for combat training: Sgt Kol Barfoot, Cpl Tosio and J T Evans *(Cpl G Iverson ABiPP)*

'The enemy will not be predictable, he won't care how he wins'. Underlying the comment was the sentiment that chivalry is preserved for the defeated opponent, not proffered to the one who is trying to kill you. Consequently, the young pilot is taught to use his skills and initiative in the elements of the day. Glaring sun in a bright blue sky? Use it to blind the opponent. A stiff breeze and white capped waves? Get down over them and lose yourself in natural camouflage. And always: it is not a game; not a flying club. Again and again, one wonders what the impact on pilot loss rate would have been in 1940 if they had received such rigorous preparation for their Hurricane and Spitfire cockpits.

Flight Lieutenant Gosling echoed several of Flight Lieutenant Cook's sentiments, in particular the physical and psychological impact of a hard combat manoeuvring sortie on a young pilot's ability to make the transition from the 'hostile' environment to a 'routine' recovery to base. 'They may become so involved with the combat that they will forget their fuel state. They may have narrowly avoided collision or they may have 'crashed' below the simulated ground height at 10,000 feet. They may have lost a rare opportunity of 'killing' an instructor by misjudging their closing speed, overshooting their 'target' and leaving themselves dead in his gun sights. They then may be called upon to lead their battle formation back to base, perhaps through low cloud. 'We see some interesting recoveries sometimes', concluded Flight Lieutenant Gosling with a certain amount of understatement.

A frequent observation by fighter pilots engaged in air-to-air combat in 1940, and in more recent conflicts in the Middle and Far East is that you never see the man who shoots you down. Flight Lieutenant Gosling gave a further little insight into that frequently fatal circumstance. Even if the pilot is not glancing at his fuel guage or distracted in some other way, he may lose sight of his target as it evades and he executes a high G turn to manoeuvre to follow it. At first he will not have the experience to look where he should expect it to reappear, 'They lose tally, they fail to remember where he was, where he is likely to be now. There's an awful lot of sky out there.' Under such circumstances, the excellent all-round vision afforded by the Spitfire's bubble canopy, compared to the metal framework over the ME 109 pilot was often a priceless advantage. And in 1940, the novice pilot was not trying to get the better of one hard-nosed but ultimately friendly QWI, but as likely as not several ME 109s all bent on his destruction. How long does it take to develop situational awareness? Flight Lieutenant Gosling's reply might have been disheartening had it been overheard by his students: 'A lot of hours; even after my front line squadron experience, I became a far better combat pilot when I came to Chivenor to teach it.'

If Britain's air defence should ever be tested in war again, the flow of novice pilots to the front line would be slowed down because a proportion of the four squadrons at Brawdy and Chivenor would assume their war role of day fighter equipped with guns and AIM 9L all aspect heat-seeking air-to-air missiles. Sixty Hawks would join the front line in Britain, and a further 12 would deploy to the Central Region of Europe. Nos 63 and 151 Squadrons from Chivenor both have distinguished squadron histories. No 63 was formed at Stirling in 1916 and moved to the Middle East where it fought against the Turks in Mesopotamia. Disbanded after the war, it reformed in 1937 as a light bomber training unit. Later, it flew tactical reconnaissance with Mustangs, Hurricanes and Spitfires, subsequently converting to the post-war Meteor and Hunter. Since 1966, it has served at Brawdy and Chivenor with a peacetime combat training role ready to supplement the front line fighter squadrons with a considerable wealth of pilot experience.

151 Squadron was formed at Hainault Farm in Essex in June 1918, equipped with Sopwith Camels to become the RAF's first dedicated night fighter/intruder squadron. Although operational in France for only five months, and flying at night without night flying instruments or target location aids, the squadron destroyed 26 enemy bombers: an outstanding achievement.

Disbanded with the majority of RAF squadrons after the war, it was reformed in 1936 during the period of rapid expansion after the identification of the imminent threat from Hitler's Germany. In December 1938, it received the Hurricane I and by September

Engine change for a 63 Sqn Hawk at Chivenor *(Cpl G Iverson ABiPP)*

1939 was in position at North Weald. From forward detachments at Manston, aircraft flew over northern France to support the handful of fighter squadrons deployed to assist the British Expeditionary Force. It flew patrols over Dunkirk and thereafter, alongside the other squadrons of 11 Group, it experienced the ever increasing combat tempo of July and August engaged in the thick of the fighting over south-east England. It accounted for 38 German aircraft but at a cost of steadily increasing losses itself. In the last seven days of August alone, 151 lost 12 Hurricanes, four pilots killed and five injured. On 1 September, it was withdrawn by Air Marshal Dowding to regroup and re-equip to the relative calm of Digby in Lincolnshire. It was however soon back in action during the Blitz and subsequently flew Mosquito night fighters over Britain, the western Atlantic and on intruder operations

over Germany. Disbanded in 1946, it reformed in 1951 at Leuchars, again for the night fighter role. It has been located at Chivenor since 1981.

The two squadrons at Brawdy are Nos 79 and 234. No 79 was formed at Gosport in August 1917, moved to France and, by the end of the war, was credited with 64 German aircraft destroyed. Disbanded in 1919 it was reformed at the time of the rapid pre-war fighter squadron expansion in 1937, re-equipping with Hurricanes at Biggin Hill in November 1938. It deployed forward to France in early May 1940 and fought incessantly thereafter for two months until, on 10 July, the exhausted squadron was removed from the front line at Hawkinge to rest and train replacement pilots at Turnhouse in Scotland. Ironically, despite its constant combat, No 79 would not have won Battle of Britain honours had it not later moved back south, because 10 July was the 'official' opening date of the battle. The 'resting' continued at Acklington, where to the pilot's great satisfaction, they frequently interrupted the activities of *Luftflotte* 5 from Norway. On 27 August, they returned to Biggin Hill to join the most critical phase of the Battle until the first massive raid against London on 7 September. Then they began their first association with the Principality when they were switched to Pembrey to protect the south west against increasing Luftwaffe attacks on industrial targets. Over the previous 12 months the squadron had suffered heavily, but the cost to the Luftwaffe was even higher: 76 confirmed kills and 44 other 'probables'. Disbanded in 1945, the squadron saw fighter-reconnaissance service in Germany before returning to Brawdy with the Hawk, in 1974.

No 234 Squadron had an unusual beginning for a unit which was also to earn great distinction as a fighter squadron in 1940. It was formed at Trescoe in the Scilly Isles in February 1917 as a Royal Naval Air Service anti-submarine flying boat squadron, assuming the number plate 234 in the creation of the RAF on 1 April 1918. Disbanded in 1919, it reformed in October 1939 at Leconfield with a mixed bag of Blenheims, Magisters, Tutors, Gauntlets and Battles. In March 1940, it moved to front line status with the Spitfire and from June until the end of the Battle it fought the Luftwaffe over southern England and the Channel from St Eval in Cornwall and Middle Wallop in Hampshire. On 4 September the squadron's records note the highest score of any squadron in one engagement: 14 ME 110s and 1 Do.17. In the post-war jet era, 234 flew Vampires, Sabres and Hunters, being associated with the Hunter OCU at Chivenor in 1958. Like No, 79, 234 Squadron moved with its Hawks to Brawdy in 1974.

The combined war-time contribution by the Hawks from Chivenor and Brawdy, supplemented by the RAF Red Arrow aerobatic team, would be a significant addition to the all-weather Tornadoes and Phantoms. The TWU pilots sustain a high level of combat skills by virtue of their training role and participation in large-scale exercises. They would either fly with their all weather colleagues as a mixed

Mixed fighter force: Tornado and Hawk on Combat Air Patrol *(Sqn Ldr T R Paxton)*

fighter force or operate independently under close ground control, probably at low level where the aircraft's agility would be of greatest value in short range missile and gun combat. Overall, the Hawk 'package' offers the air defence commander a readily available, highly skilled reinforcement to his front line in times of crisis, of a kind which could never be made available in 1940.

Navigators

In 1940, all the front line squadrons, with the exception of the Blenheims and Defiants, were equipped with single seat aircraft. Consequently, pilots bore the overwhelming brunt of the Battle. In 1990, all the front line fighters are flown by a pilot and navigator, only the reinforcing Hawks, although two seat, would have a single crew member. As will be seen later, the fighter pilot and fighter navigator come together as a team at the OCU. Meanwhile the 'ab initio' fast jet back-seater has been pursuing a complementary training path.

Like his pilot colleague he will be a commissioned officer. With the advent of fast jet aircraft many years ago, the RAF came to believe that the additional responsibilities demanded from the crews merited the higher status and better pay of the commissioned officer. There are many who would argue that similar grounds could well have been made on behalf of the Sergeant Pilots who fought in 1940, among them Sergeant Neil Cameron, later Marshal of the Royal Air Force Sir Neil Cameron, or Sergeant J H (Ginger) Lacey, or Sergeant Josef Frantisek whose 17 victories in September made him the RAF's joint top scoring pilot of the Battle. Now, however, all pilots and navigators begin their commissioned careers as graduates from the Initial Officer Training Course at Cranwell. Thereafter, while the pilots move to one of the three Basic Flying Training Schools, the navigators move down the road to Finningley, near Doncaster to begin their own professional training.

All will complete ground school, 70 hours on the twin engined Dominie, 20 hours in the back seat of a Jet Provost and 50 in the simulator learning the basics of timing, fuel calculations, diversions and the air navigation systems common to most modern military aircraft. At this stage the students, like their pilot colleagues, will be separated into two seat fast jet and multi-engined streams. The former, from whom the Air Defence navigator will ultimately be selected, will complete a further advanced 25 hours on the Dominie and 15 on the Jet Provost learning to handle radar at low level, target approaches and formation techniques at 300 knots at 250 feet. The future air defence navigators complete the advanced phase with an introduction to basic air combat training, low level visual intercepts and Ground Control Intercepts (GCI) with a GCI station. From there they go to Chivenor or Brawdy to gain experience in the back seat of the high speed, highly manoeuvrable Hawk which demands, for the first time, a sustained tactical awareness while suffering the discomfort of frequent and often unpredictable heavy G loading. They are encouraged to begin to think as part of a two man team: to retain a mental air picture, to monitor pilot instruments at critical points in manoeuvre and to be aware of what information the combat pilot will need, and when. They have embarked on the transition from theoretical navigator to combat team members. It is a journey which, if successful, can lead them up equal rungs of promotion with the pilots to Squadron Commander, Station Commander and ultimately air rank. For many of them, it seems a long and uncomfortable way away as they experience their first series of low level high G turns at 400 knots over the Devon hills. By the time they arrive at their next destination, Leuchars or Coningsby, they will be acclimatised.

The Operational Conversion Units

At this stage, pilot and navigator are ready to convert to either the Tornado or Phantom. The two 11 Group Phantom squadrons are fed by No 228 OCU at Leuchars, which also provides crews for Nos 19 and 92, based at Wildenwrath in Germany. The Tornado crews go to No 229 OCU at Coningsby, where they will spend about four months mastering the F3 before they either move across the airfield to one of the squadrons on the Coningsby wing or join colleagues at Leuchars or Leeming.

No 229 OCU

Flight Commander (Training) on the 229 OCU is Squadron Leader Chris Smith, a navigator with 1700 total air defence hours, 350 of them on the F3. He explained in great detail the way in which the young pilots and navigators progress from basic flying skills to a level of competence on the F3 necessary to take their place in the front line squadrons.

The newcomers spend two weeks learning the basics of the air defence world such as interpreting radar displays, techniques of 180° and 90° intercepts and shadowing. They then move to the four-week ground school phase of the main course in which they will become familiar with the systems on the aircraft. With the aid of simulation they will work as a crew for the first time, becoming used to the Head Up display, cockpit emergencies, missile management and avionics. They will complete six checkrides in the mission simulator, and in the final one 'anything can happen'. Then it is out to the aircraft. The pilot will fly sorties first with a QFI in the back and will normally go solo with a staff navigator after about five hours. Meanwhile the navigator will fly with a staff pilot and begin to appreciate the speed of reaction needed from the backseater. The actual navigation, because of the refined aircraft instruments, is relatively straightforward but he must learn to monitor the various management systems and become aware of the prospect of swiftly changing tactical situations. The first solo flown by the student crew is a major milestone, and one carefully monitored by the staff because, as yet, the pilot does not have his instrument rating. Consequently, the staff will pay particular attention to the meteorological conditions along the proposed route. Then, after further dual rides with a QFI, in which the young pilot practises instrument flying at night also, he is shown the limits of the aircraft and learns to handle the Tornado in close formation. Then, having stepped onto the instrument rating ladder with his 'white card', having passed an instrument rating test after about 16 hours, he is ready to take his navigator into the next four weeks, known as the Basic Radar Phase. In this, the crew come to grips with head-on and stern engagements, taking it in turns with another Tornado to be interceptor and target. First one on one, then one against

Tornado F3 of No 229 OCU: crew preparing for sortie *(SACW Julie-Ann Timbrell)*

two, which represents another step forward because they have to organise attacks which would kill both targets, with about one minute in which to decide how to do it, and two to execute both attacks. At the end of this phase, which usually takes about 13½ hours they will be expected to intercept pairs of aircraft which could be evading at low level. In those circumstances, the staff will have been particularly monitoring the trainee crews' ability to develop the spare capacity to handle the aircraft progressively down to 250 feet above the sea. The next, Combat Phase, leads the crew through the complexities of radar engagement working as a pair, first against singleton targets. A Qualified Weapons Instructor (QWI) will introduce the trainee to aggressive combat manoeuvring: basic fighter tactics adding visual engagements to initial radar positioning from distances up to 40 miles. Finally, in this

phase, the pilot will learn how to control his own aircraft and communicate his intention to a colleague: the basis of his future squadron day to day 'pairs' activity. In the combat phase, the pilot will fly 10, and the navigator eight training sorties.

In the last four week phase, the crew take a further major step as they begin flying low level intercepts over land at over 600 miles an hour. The targets will now be manoeuvring fully and providing a counter threat. There may also be other aircraft at low level and so situation awareness is absolutely vital.

Finally, after 50 pilot and 40 navigator hours, the crew come to their end of course checkride, which could involve them flying with a colleague against any kind of combination of low level 'attackers'. They could include Jaguars, Tornado GR1s, Hawks and other Tornado F3s', as well as ECM Canberras from Wyton. In sum, they could be called upon to apply everything they have learned over four months in one sortie.

The long course for the 'ab initios', and slightly shorter one for experienced pilots and navigators moving for the first time to the F3, are the bread and butter of 229 OCU but the staff also run two courses a year for QWIs, another for squadron Instrument Rating Examiners (IRE) and also train crews for foreign air forces such as the Royal Saudi Air Force, which also flies the F3.

In war, the aircraft and crew of the OCU would become No 65 Squadron which had a very distinguished record in the Battle of Britain. It flew Spitfires with the Hornchurch wing but spent most of the battle deployed alongside 74 Squadron at Manston. By the time it was withdrawn to rest and regroup at Church Fenton on 27 August, it had lost two squadron commanders and was down to nine serviceable aircraft and 12 battle hardened but exhausted pilots. In return, it had exacted a heavy toll on the incoming bombers and their ME 109 escorts.

No 228 OCU

Further north, at Leuchars, aircrew for the Phantom force are prepared by the officers of No 228 OCU. The accumulated experience of the instructors reflects the extent of the F4s contribution to United Kingdom air defence over several years. At the end of 1989, the OCU was commanded by Wing Commander John Walmsley with 4,200 flying hours, of which 3,000 were on the F4. The Standards Evaluation officer for both the OCU and the first line Phantom squadrons was Squadron Leader Andy Bateman: 3,000 hours and 1,300

Left: All weather in the weather: Tornado F3 of No 229 OCU *(Author)*
Above: A Tornado of the Central Tactics and Trials Organisation, attached to the Tornado Operational Evaluation Unit at Coningsby, is given a weapons system master test by Chief Technician Mick Everett *(Author)*

on the F4. Flight Lieutenant Phil Williamson, staff pilot, 4,900 hours with 3,600 of them on the Phantom. A typical OCU 'ab initio' on the other hand was Flying Officer Ian Dingwall who, in climbing the hurdles at Cranwell, Valley and Chivenor, had accumulated 120 fast jet hours and was about to add another 60 hours 'on type' during his stay at Leuchars.

In 1940 the pilots came from all walks of life: apprentice, bank clerk, public school boy, university graduate. They had many things in common with their successors of 1990, not least being the fact that it doesn't matter who you are, what you did or which school you went to, but how good you are once you don the light blue uniform. Of the four officers named above, two are university graduates, one is a direct entry grammar school boy and the fourth aspired to be a fighter pilot while he was finding time to be a distinguished member of his Air Training Corps squadron while working for his A levels.

The Leuchars course follows similar principles to that of No 229 OCU at Coningsby: preparing the young fast jet aircrew by stages for the demands of the combat squadron. Beginning with an introductory ground school, where a simplified but realistic Air Intercept Trainer and simulator prepares the way for the far more complex Phantom cockpit, the crews first become familiar with the general handling of the aircraft, then to practice intercepts one on one, air combat one on one and two on one. Practice intercepts with Phantoms are all very well, but the F4 is the last kind of target to be expected in real combat, and so 'dissimilar' training with other aircraft, as at Coningsby, plays an increasingly important part in the OCU syllabus. Gradually the complexity of the training increases: low level, high speed evading targets over land, close formation at night and, unlike No 229 OCU, one sortie to gain experience of inflight refuelling, in flights lasting from 30 minutes to two hours. After four months the 'ab initios' will either move to Wattisham or across the Channel to Wildenwrath.

They and their colleagues from Coningsby emerge from the OCUs with a healthy regard for the demands of their new environment, justifiably proud of their progress. But as yet, their skills are raw and they will find that day to day 'continuation' training on the front line,

with steady further progression to combat readiness requires many more hours of dedicated flying. But they are enjoying a luxury not known by their predecessors of 1940. The Hurricane and Spitfire pilots were expected to master their aircraft and develop their combat skills in an environment where shortfalls in competence would not be met by the firm encouragement of a training officer or QWI, but by pain or death at the hands of Luftwaffe veterans.

If the recently converted Phantom crews should be committed to combat they, like their F3 colleagues, would find their ex-instructors from the OCU alongside them. In war, 228 OCU would become No 64 Squadron and, like the translation of No 229 OCU to 65, the number is well chosen. 64 Squadron had been re-formed after a long absence at the time of the Abyssinian crisis of 1935. By 1 July 1940, it was equipped with Spitfires, based at Kenley and shared the first kill of that month, a Dornier 17, with Hurricanes of 145 Squadron from Tangmere. In view of the modern peacetime role of 64 Squadron it is sadly ironic to read how in those early days of July sustained patrols by the 11 Group fighters, the vast majority over the sea in poor weather, not only took a steady toll of the pilots but also restricted training of the 'ab initios' with inevitable results when the combat intensified. Yet while training might have been sparse, there was fighter pilot aggression in abundance. On 25 July for example, Squadron Leader Aeneas MacDonnell led eight Spitfires into attack against 30 JU 88s and 50 escorting ME 109s over a British convoy in the Straits of Dover. Supported by 11 Hurricanes from 111 Squadron and three reinforcements from Kenley, the Spitfires broke up the JU 88s and the ME 109s disengaged. Measured against the millions who died in the Second World War the losses of 64 Squadron that afternoon were not high: two pilots killed and one safely crash landed. But both were very experienced; one of them, Sub-Lieutenant F Dawson-Paul already had five kills and was representative of many naval pilots who had been transferred to the RAF during the previous 12 months to meet the desperate shortage.

For two months, 64 Squadron operated in the thick of the Battle from Kenley, reporting almost daily tallies of hostile aircraft damaged and destroyed, until in the last week of August it too was withdrawn to the relative tranquility of Leconfield; happily, still led by Squadron Leader MacDonnell, whose subsequent distinguished career was to take him to air rank in the post-war RAF.

Perhaps, in the old soldier's adage, there is no substitute for combat experience, but at least in 1990 the inexperienced pilot goes to his new squadron with as comprehensive a preparation as peacetime can provide. The staff crews of Nos 228 and 229 OCU would not require any refresher flying to prepare them for combat. In 1940, on many occasions the well known Luftwaffe warning '*Achtung Spitfire*' was prompted by the sight of the pilots of 64 and 65 Squadrons; in any future conflict involving them there would be no novices in the cockpits.

Tactical Evaluation and Development

In 1940, a Royal Air Force Manual of Air Tactics formed the basis of combat training for the Battle of Britain crews. In 1990, all units in 11 Group receive copies of '*The 11 Group Air Defence Annual Training Syllabus*.' Its objectives are 'To maintain the highest possible level of aircrew combat ready proficiency within the available flying effort' and 'To enable HQ 11 Group to monitor the training progress'. Responsibility for ensuring that each pilot and navigator completes the training exercises commensurate with his operational category is delegated to the squadron commander. Completion of the syllabus will only take up a proportion of the annual flying hours allocated to a squadron. The remainder will be consumed by large scale exercises and trials, air tests and specific extra training to meet local needs identified by the squadron commander.

The syllabus covers all aspects of the air defence task in considerable detail, including intercepts, combat air patrols, electronic warfare, inflight refuelling, emergency procedures and various levels of instrument rating requirement. Further classified documents relate the training guidelines to the aircraft characteristics and tactics likely to be employed by a potential enemy in war. The tenor of the 11 Group Syllabus may be grasped from a footnote to Air Combat Exercise No 5: 'The

purpose of AC5 is to give the crews experience of attacking an aircraft in a hostile environment where another hostile may well be about to attack them . . .' Or from the guideline on Formation Flying: 'The roles of the squadron of No 11 Group demand that sufficient practice is obtained to ensure proficiency in close, battle, and AI snake formation. It is particularly important for pilots to be proficient in formation recoveries under instrument conditions.'

In 1990, the aircraft and tactics of a potential enemy are likely to be well known. Even when an unexpected enemy appears, as in the Falklands in 1982, the performance of his aircraft, now produced by a handful of major aerospace companies worldwide, will come as no surprise. Foreign combat training and recent combat experience in the Third World are assiduously studied by operational and intelligence staffs to reduce, as far as possible, the element of either technological or tactical surprise at the outbreak of war.

Responsiveness to the activities of a potential enemy is however only part of the task of operational preparation. One wishes a potential enemy to have to worry about one's own tactical innovation and that means constantly evaluating, re-evaluating and developing, so that tactical initiative and surprise will be on your side, not his.

In 1940, good aeroplanes were equipping Fighter Command squadrons, leadership was strong and a rudimentary but effective ground warning and control system was in position. Tactics, however, were outdated; devised for a different strategic environment to meet a different kind of air attack from that actually faced. No one had foreseen the rapidity of the collapse of western Europe in the face of the German Blitzkreig. The air staff had identified Germany as the potential enemy, but had expected to defend British skies against formations of poorly manoeuvrable bombers escorted, if at all, by small numbers of fighters at the limits of their combat radius. Before the war, the British Air Staff, along with most of their contemporaries, believed that bomber squadrons with heavy mutually supporting firepower would be very difficult to intercept. As a result British fighter pilots were trained to intercept in tight formations where station keeping was very important. A squadron for-

Cpl Mick Storey changing a main power amplifier in a Phantom missile control system, on No 228 OCU at Leuchars *(Author)*

mation would comprise four closely-spaced sections of three aircraft each and the actual profile would be selected and called over the R/T by the squadron leader. The attack manoeuvre would be identified by a drill number taken from a list of 'Fighting Area Attacks', and could include a sequential attack by all 12 fighters against one nominated bomber. As the fighter pilots were trained to open fire between 300 and 400 yards and then breakaway because of the perceived threat from the bombers' own guns, there would not necessarily be the degree of overkill which the theoretical drill suggested.

But the Luftwaffe did not have to fly several hundred miles from German bases, and the ME 109s, either as escorts or 'free hunting' for RAF fighters, quickly took advantage of pilots who were preoccupied with station keeping at the cost of wider look-out and who had been taught to attack by numbers. The ME 109s flew as a *Staffel*, or flight of eight or nine fighters, in widely spaced *Schwarmen* or pairs, depending on the tactical appreciation of the pilots at the time.

There was no time for the RAF pilots to reflect on their tactical obsolescence, issue a new manual and standardise squadron response. No directives were issued and individual squadron commanders were forced to improvise. Some, like Squadron Leader

Thompson of 111 Squadron, led his Hurricanes head on into attack, which had a devastating impact on the incoming bomber squadrons, but ultimately led to too great a price being paid in air-to-air collisions. Others, such as Squadron Leader Devitt of 152 Squadron, devised his own system of pairs, dividing his Spitfires into six sections, with a leader and a No 2 comprising a fighting unit with the leader taking offensive action and the No 2 providing defensive cover. But squadron response was piecemeal, and naturally so when new pilots arrived after receiving the old tactical training and experienced pilots were flying up to four sorties a day. This is the detail behind the strategic threat to Fighter Command posed by the Luftwaffe concentration in late August and early September 1940. Not just constant pressure, constant combat, survival and losses, but the denial of any opportunity to pause, take stock and revise tactics which were demonstrably obsolete, inferior and all too often fatal.

The Tornado F3 Operational Evaluation Unit

Military history is replete with victors in war who were well satisfied with their successes, rested on their laurels, failed to analyse weaknesses concealed among their strengths and were, as a result, roundly defeated in subsequent combat by more analytical and perceptive opponents. One significant legacy of the Battle of Britain is that victory, heroism and justifiable pride have not obscured that fundamental need for objective analysis and, most importantly, constant re-evaluation of modern fighter tactics.

In an adjacent hangar to No 229 OCU at Coningsby is the Tornado F3 Operational Evaluation Unit (OEU), usually comprising three aircraft and a handful of extremely experienced fighter specialists, led by Wing Commander Mal Gleave. Since joining the RAF in 1965, Wing Commander Gleave has accumulated a formidable depth and breadth of experience on which to base his credibility in his present appointment. During tours on Lightnings in Britain and Germany he became a QWI in 1971. He taught USAF weapon instructors at Tyndall Air Force Base, where he flew the F106 and participated in weapon research and development, working also with American ground control systems. He flew F4s with 11 Squadron, taught air defence tactics on the Royal Navy's maritime tactical course at HMS *Dryad*, attended the RAF Staff College, spent a tour of duty with the RAF's Central Tactics and Trials Organisation (CTTO) as air defence specialist, did a spell as air defence staff officer in the Falklands, began flying the F2 in 1986 and since 1987 has led the F3 OEU.

The OEU is responsible for the progressive evolution of the F3 weapon system, aircraft and tactics in an operational environment. Wing Commander Gleave is tasked by the Assistant Chief of the Air Staff through CTTO with specific responsibilities to 'Develop operational tactics for Tornado F3; Maintain the CTTO F3 tactics manual; Plan, execute and report F3 trials; Propose modifications and trials to enhance F3 effectiveness and liaise with staff, squadrons, the Aeroplane and Armament Experimental Establishment at Boscombe Down, and Industry.'

Wing Commander Gleave explained the rationale behind the creation of his specialist unit: 'We need to establish the knowledge which doesn't come with a new aircraft. The difference between exercises and the real thing is that in training you construct the scenario; in real life you can't, so you must look at all the possibilities. Operational tactics are of the greatest importance. We had to devise trials to find out what the aircraft could do, beginning with basic tasks e.g. Combat Air Patrols, examining the air breathing threat at various levels and the impact of different kinds of electronic counter and counter-counter measures. We now have an aircraft which can operate across the UKADR from bases in either sector and therefore we must also examine the large scale options and battle plan implications for the Air Defence Commander. In addition to the very different capabilities of the F3 itself, we have to take into account changes in the perceived threat, the proximity to service of the E3D Sentry, the onset of widespread, secure, real time communications and a new generation of beyond-visual-range air-to-air weapons.'

A survey of some of the detailed subjects which Wing Commander Gleave's team has to consider illustrates most dramatically how much more complex the air defence environment has become since 1940. He works closely with the operational research staff at Headquarters Strike Command on statistical surveys across the Tornado fleet drawn from post sortie reports to monitor the performance of weapons systems and ECCM equipment. Surprise remains a powerful advantage in air combat and so not only must the OEU be concerned with the F3's ability to intercept opponents, but also with its own degree of visibility as it does so. Visual characteristics, radar cross sections and infra-red emissions are all factors to be meticulously examined. Sometimes requirements can be contradictory, as Wing Commander Gleave explained: 'The ability to pull high G is valuable for manoeuvring, but you could at the same time present a large radar cross section and a high IR signature to another opponent; it's the junior pilot popping out of the cloud who says "Thanks very much"'.

Soviet aircraft have become more capable and the Soviet Air Force has begun to experiment with formations of bombers escorted by long range fighters, the whole package being enshrouded in electronic warfare support. Whatever the nature and source of future air threats to the United Kingdom, the need to counter such combinations of high performance, well armed and EW-capable aircraft will continue. Consequently there will be continued emphasis on front hemisphere beyond-visual-range (BVR) missile engagement supplemented by shorter range all aspect attack infra-red (IR) weapons and guns, in tactics which can be applied at night and in all weathers.

Wing Commander Gleave has access not only to senior staffs, but directly to the manufacturers of the aircraft and weapons and to the crews who are flying the F3 daily. The OEU is the pivotal point in the communications and a visible guarantee that no one is going to make the mistake of 1940 of sending aircrew into combat with tactics which are obsolete, or impracticable, or both. Closing the loop, the work of the OEU is designed to ensure that even before they reach their front line squadrons, the Tornado crew will receive realistic and regularly updated operational training.

Chapter Three

THE FRONT LINE SQUADRONS

O N 15 SEPTEMBER 1940, there were 68 squadrons listed in the Bentley Priory order of battle. Fifty years later there are 9 front line squadrons which would be complemented in war by the two squadrons formed from the OCUs and the four from the TWUs.

The nine front line squadrons are distributed in peacetime on four major operating bases down the eastern half of the United Kingdom. Nos 43 and 111 squadrons share RAF Leuchars with No 228 OCU. Nos 11, 23 and 25 are based at RAF Leeming in North Yorkshire. Nos 5 and 29 share RAF Coningsby in Lincolnshire with No 229 OCU, and Nos 56 and 74 fly from RAF Wattisham near Ipswich in Suffolk.

In 1940 the British 'front line' was south-east England, the closest point to German squadrons on the continent. In the long confrontation with the Soviet Union and her Warsaw Pact allies, the shortest route from Warsaw Pact territory has been either round or across the North Cape from airfields in the Kola peninsula of north-west Russia to north-east England and Scotland: hence the geographical location of the main air defence bases.

The Leuchars Wing

The northernmost base, Leuchars in Fife, was a Coastal Command station in 1940; now it is the home of two squadrons which fought in the battle in south-east England. The older of the two is No 43 – 'The Fighting Cocks', named after their squadron emblem, the Game Cock. 43 has a long association with Scotland, being formed at Stirling on 15 April 1916. In France it flew Sopwith Strutters, Camels and Snipes in fighter, reconnaissance and ground attack duties. In the inter-war years, it was based in south-east England, re-equipping with Hurricane I in 1938, moving first to Acklington and then to Wick in the early months of the war. At the end of May 1940, it returned to Tangmere, joining the combat patrols over the Dunkirk beaches. On 1 July, 43 had 13 Hurricanes serviceable and four unserviceable as they began daily interceptions of the still spasmodic and uncoordinated German attacks against British shipping. By 23 July, although there had been no decisive air battles, 43 Squadron had lost six pilots, including one squadron commander and one flight commander and was withdrawn to RAF Northolt to train new pilots. It is significant that in this period the skies round Northolt were considered safe enough for such a purpose. Eight days later the 'training' was complete, and 18 serviceable Hurricanes returned to Tangmere. Routine missions were flown for a week as the Luftwaffe prepared for its major onslaught. From 8 August to 7 September, 43 Squadron flew continuously, losing a further squadron commander and several squadron pilots.

In the fighter squadrons, losses were counted in twos and threes, numerically insignificant when compared say to the loss of 60,000 aircrew in the Bomber Command, or the hundreds of thousands at Stalingrad. But it was a personal war, epitomised by the loss on 2 September of Pilot Officer C A Wood-Scawen in combat with ME109s over Ashford. 24 hours earlier his elder brother, Flying Officer P P Wood-Scawen of 85 Squadron had been shot down by another ME109 over Kenley and died when his parachute failed to open.

On 8 September, the exhausted squadron was withdrawn from the front line by the Commander-in-Chief and moved to Usworth in Northumberland. It took eight days to make 11 Hurricanes sufficiently air-worthy to attempt the ferry flight northwards. Since then, with the exception of a couple of short periods when it was awaiting aircraft, 43 has seen unbroken service as a fighter squadron, serving for most of the post war period at Leuchars. The Hunter of the 1950s and 1960s was followed by the F4 Phantom, until final conversion to Tornado F3 in early 1990.

The second Leuchars squadron, 111, known familiarly as 'Treble One', had a very similar and equally distinguished combat record in the Battle of Britain. After early service in the Middle East, 111 began unbroken fighter service in south-east England in 1923. It was the first squadron to be equipped with the Hurricane I in December 1937, and also moved north on the outbreak of war. It then operated in France and over Dunkirk. On 1 July 1940 it had 12 Hurricanes serviceable and four unserviceable (U/S), at Kenley. In the following weeks the squadron achieved tactical

surprise on several occasions by formation head on attacks on bomber squadrons. Not surprisingly the Luftwaffe pilots took rapid evasive action, breaking down their defensive cohesion, losing track and, if close to their target, also their bombing line.

In 1940, gunnery regulations specified that fire from the wing-mounted machine-guns should converge at 650 yards range but many pilots instructed their armourers to synchronise convergence at much less than that. In a head on attack, of course, range considerations were rather more academic, but closing speeds in excess of 600 miles an hour between two formations inevitably increased the incidence of air-to-air collision. So much so, that Treble One was forced to abandon the tactic, losing too many experienced pilots. In 1990, the head on attack is once more a standard tactic, with the advent of radar guided missiles launched beyond visual range, and heat-seeking, all-aspect shorter range weapons. Now however, the distances at missile launch are such that air-to-air collisions are readily avoidable.

During July and August 1940, Treble One was deployed on various 11 Group airfields: Kenley, Croydon, Martlesham Heath and theoretically 'resting' at Debden, but their

Right: Newly arrived on the Squadron: Tornado F3 of No 43 Squadron *(No 43 Squadron/Crown Copyright)*
Below right: The squadron 'flagship' of No 111 Squadron, just before conversion to Tornado in 1989 *(No 111 Squadron/Crown Copyright)*

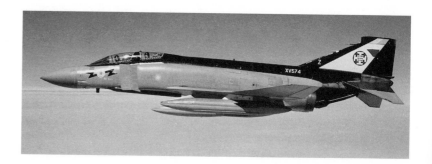

daily routine was the same. Usually called around 3 a.m. for first light standby, then sorties as required until twilight some 19 hours later, alongside the other Hurricane and Spitfire squadrons. Treble One was fortunate in that the squadron commander appointed on 1 July, Squadron Leader J M Thompson, survived over two months of continuous combat and contributed greatly to the sustained fighting cohesion of the squadron. With a CBE, DSO, DFC and Bar he ultimately attained Air rank. He was typical of those who met the RAF requirement, still demanded in 1990, for a squadron commander to lead by example, in the air and on the ground.

No 111 was finally withdrawn from the Battle on 8 September, the same day as 43, and sent north to Drem in Scotland to train new pilots and recuperate from the impact of almost four months of incessant combat. In 1943 and 1944, it flew alongside 43 Squadron again in Italy, and since 1945, like 43, has always been in fighter service except for short periods before acquiring new aircraft types. Treble One has been based at Leuchars since 1975, equipped first with F4 Phantoms and converting to Tornado F3s in 1990.

The Leeming Wing

Leeming, in north Yorkshire is the only one of the four main fighter bases of 1990 to have had a direct association with the Battle of Britain. Originally an airfield belonging to Yorkshire Air Services, it became a bomber base in 1940. But it was also a satellite field for 13 Group's Catterick Wing, and in the Fighter Command Order of Battle of 1 August, it is shown as the home of 15 night-fighter Blenheims of 219 Squadron. In 1990, the drone of the Bristol Mercuries has been replaced by the roar of the Rolls Royce RB.199s of the Tornado F3.

The most senior of the Leeming squadrons is No 11, bearing a distinguished list of battle honours since its formation at Netheravon in February 1915. Engaged in fighter and reconnaissance duties in France, it returned for a short spell in Britain in the 1920s before moving to India in 1928. Subsequently, operations were unusually varied, ranging from primitive expeditions against marauding tribesmen in the North-West Frontier Province to trial reinforcement flights to Singapore. Fortunately for the squadron, but not for the island, No 11 did not remain to contribute to the defence of Singapore, but was brought back to the Middle East in 1940 as the German–Italian threat darkened over North Africa. The squadron thereafter saw continuous combat, equipped with Blenheims, from bases in Egypt, Greece, Palestine, Iraq and then back to India where, in 1943, it re-equipped with Hurricanes. In 1944, it flew close support missions for General Slim's 14th Army, contributing at very short order to the battle of Imphal, which took place close to the squadron's airfield. After the war, it flew from occupied bases in Japan before being disbanded in 1948, reforming later the same year as a Mosquito fighter-bomber unit at Wahn in Germany. In 1950 it re-equipped with Vampires. It has been a fighter squadron ever since, flying the Lightning for over 20 years. In 1989 the squadron re-equipped with Tornadoes. Its arrival at Leeming marked the return of the airfield to its fighter operations of 1940.

No 23 Squadron, the second senior squadron at Leeming, saw its first air defence operations while still working up after its formation at Gosport on 1 September 1915. Then, there was no organised provision for United Kingdom defence and aircraft were called in from several sources, including Gosport, to defend London against German air attack. There was little success, and indeed the continued apparent impunity with which German bombers arrived over the capital and elsewhere in Britain ultimately prompted the creation of a committee in 1917, under General Smuts, to examine the whole of the air war effort against Germany. His famous report led directly to the creation of the independent Royal Air Force in April 1918. The air defence of the United Kingdom has been a primary task of the RAF ever since.

In company with the other early squadrons of the RFC, 23 Squadron quickly moved across to France carrying out fighter, reconnaissance and ground attack operations. After a brief period of disbandment at the end of the war, it reformed at Henlow, remaining in the south of England until 1937. The threat from Hitler's Germany was apparent, and the late decision in 1936 to accelerate fighter produc-

Preparing to scramble: Squadron Leader Ted Threapleton and Flight Lieutenant Mark Fessey with their No 11 Squadron Tornado in the QRA HAS at Leeming *(Author)*

F3 of No 23 Squadron with in-flight refuelling probe extended *(Sqn Ldr T R Paxton)*

tion was beginning to take effect, but production of both Spitfire and Hurricane was running behind schedule. In the prevous year, however, the twin engined Blenheim light bomber had entered service in Bomber Command. It had a speed – close to 300 mph – range, manoeuvring capability and weapon capacity, greater than the biplane fighters of that era, although not to the same degree as the ME109, which had already flown in combat with the Luftwaffe's Condor Legion in the Spanish Civil War. As a stopgap, the Blenheim was converted from bomber to fighter by the removal of bomb bay doors and the installation of a centre line, underbelly gun pack containing four .303 Browning machine guns, in addition to the one Vickers .303 gun in the original mid-upper dorsal air gunner's turret. Such alignment reduced problems of gunfire convergence and the Blenheims 1F of No 23 Squadron were allocated a night fighter role in the Battle of Britain. Without airborne intercept radar, theirs was a thankless task and the guns were not extensively fired in anger. In December 1940, the squadron began intruder offensive counter-air operations against enemy airfields, a role which was sustained for the greater part of the war, ultimately in Mosquitoes, over Italy, France and Germany. After disbanding again after the war, 23 Squadron was reformed at Wittering – its old Battle of Britain base – as a night-fighter squadron equipped with Vampire NF10s. Since then, except for periods when preparing to receive new aircraft, it has been a night/all-weather squadron, flying Lightnings, Phantoms and, since November 1988, Tornado F3s.

The most recent addition to the Leeming Wing is No 25 Squadron, which declared its F3s operational at the beginning of 1990. The Squadron was formed at Montrose in September 1915, moving to France early the following year. For 18 months it was engaged in fighter reconnaissance operations before changing both aircraft and roles to become a DH4 daylight bombing squadron, attacking enemy airbases. In 1920, the squadron re-equipped with Sopwith Snipe fighters, based at Hawkinge, and such was the run down and overseas dispersal of the RAF after the war that, for a while, 25 Squadron was the only air defence squadron in Britain. Except for a year's detach-

ment to Turkey in 1922, the squadron continued in the air defence role until in December 1938, it too re-equipped with Blenheim 1Fs. There was, however, one vital addition to the conversion of four of 25 Squadron's Blenheims: the world's first airborne interception (AI) radar, which was fitted in November 1939. Experiments had been taking place since 1935 and by September 1937 a radar transmitter-receiver set in an Avro Anson flying from Martlesham Heath in Suffolk was receiving rudimentary reflected signal returns from both ships and aircraft.

Initially, the equipment installed in the Blenheims could give a marginal indication of a target's range, but not a bearing, but experiments continued steadily in technique and tactics. 25 Squadron contributed to the Dunkirk evacuation by flying combat patrols along the coast and providing air cover for ships returning to England.

On 1 July 1940, the squadron was deployed with 16 aircraft at Martlesham Heath in the North Weald sector, and continued working up for night interception missions. On 30 August, an ominous incident occurred when Hurricanes of 111 Squadron were scrambled against an incoming 'raid' near the Thames Estuary. The 'raid' proved to be three Blenheims from 25 Squadron returning to their new base at North Weald. Fortunately, the Treble One pilots recognised their colleagues in time. Four days later, three other Blenheims were less fortunate. During the morning of 3 September, a vast mêlée took place over Essex and Kent involving 16 fighter squadrons and a mixed force of 130 Dorniers and escorting Messerschmitt 109s and 110s. As the German formations ultimately withdrew, the three Blenheims began to return to their airfield and were mistaken for Ju 88s by Hurricanes of No 46 Squadron. One was shot down with the loss of its pilot, one was badly damaged but managed to make a forced landing at Hatfield, and the third evaded the Hurricanes and returned safely to its base. Meanwhile the 46 Squadron pilots had reported one Ju 88 destroyed and three damaged. There were no Ju 88s in the area that morning. This was not the first time, nor would it be the last, that friendly forces had fallen to colleagues' guns and incidents of 'Blue on Blue' are sadly not

Tornado F3 of 25 Squadron with wings fully forward *(Flt Lt Ian Black)*

unique to fighting in the air, nor to any one service or country. In the air, however, the problems of timely and accurate identification of friend or foe (IFF) are acute, and in different ways they remain so in 1990. In 1940 there were structural similarities between aircraft on both sides, in particular the Blenheim and the Ju 88, and at certain angles, the Spitfire and the Messerschmitt. The RAF fighters were usually outnumbered, frequently involved in multiple dogfights and split second decisions were often required whether to shoot or not. All combat was by visual contact, and by gun or cannon. IFF was primarily achieved by the eye of the pilot or air gunner although a rudimentary signal system was beginning to enter service. Everyone connected with the air war, and a high proportion of the small boy population as well, assiduously studied diagrams and photographs of British and German aircraft to be able to detect distinctive features at long range, high altitude and in bad light. Accurate aircraft recognition was the only reliable way to avoid

the tragedies of 'Blue on Blue'.

But even as the fighters of 25 Squadron began to shoot down German bombers by night – the first during the evening following the 'Ju 88' fiasco on 3 September – British scientists were examining ways of improving bombing and navigation aids and devising methods of disrupting German aircraft intercept radar (AI) and early warning systems. Across the other side of the Channel, the scientists and signals troops of General Wolfgang Martini were engaged in similar activities. A new dimension of electronic warfare was to be added to air combat. Radar had become a weapon of war, with Chain Home stations on the ground and 25 Squadron's AI-equipped Blenheims in the sky.

Fifty years later, modern technology has in its usual ambivalent way offered both a solution and a further complication to the IFF problem. The solution lay hidden in the first rudimentary equipment carried by 25 Squadron's Blenheims. Initially, the AI radar received simple reflections from a target. If, however, a specific signal from the illuminated aircraft could also be detected by the same AI equipment, then an identification code could be incorporated and the intercepting pilot would know immediately whether the intruder was indeed hostile or not. The IFF signal would be represented on the interceptor's radar screen as a 'blip' with some kind of additional shape or other distinguishing characteristic accompanying it. This basic principle has now been refined and is in operation with air forces and other users of radar equipment – including civilian authorities – world wide.

In theory, therefore, a modern fighter pilot does not need to close within visual range before firing his guided missiles. His AI radar both illuminates and interrogates the potential target, which in turn either responds with the IFF code of the day or any other identification procedure. Thereafter the situation is quite clear and the problem of 'Blue on Blue' is resolved.

In practice, however, it is not that simple. Equipment can become unserviceable. Aircraft can suffer battle damage, or indeed, in the heat and haste of combat, mistakes can be made when setting up equipment in the first place. But of more significance is the ability of electronic counter measures (ECM) to render the basic IFF procedure unreliable. AI radar, and indeed any other kind of radar, can be jammed by an opponent who can thereby render incoming signals indecipherable. Such activity would obviously indicate a hostile presence but it could also make discrimination between other aircraft much more difficult. Electronic counter counter measures (ECCM) are becoming sophisticated and the silent war between confusion and clarity will continue. More insidious than jamming however, is 'spoofing': deliberate transmission of an IFF or other signal, apparently in clear, which presents a friendly image on the AI screen. Such activity is based on awareness of an opponent's IFF procedures and codes and, not surprisingly, all information, except for basic principles, is highly classified. In sum, therefore, the aircrew of No 25 Squadron face the same basic problem of target identification as their forebears in 1940 and not all will be readily soluble by modern technology. How

another RAF squadron helps 25 and the other fighter squadrons to prepare for electronic warfare will be explained in Chapter Five.

The Coningsby Wing

The Coningsby Wing was the first in 11 Group to receive Tornado F3s in 1987. The senior squadron, No 5 completed conversion to the Tornado at the beginning of 1988 after 23 years previous experience with the Lightning at neighbouring Binbrook. No 5 was formed at Farnborough in July 1913 and since then has discharged several roles in addition to its regular commitment to fighter interception. In the First World War it was primarily a reconnaissance squadron. In 1920, at a time when many RAF squadrons were deployed around the British Empire, 5 Squadron was reconstituted at Quetta for duties in north-west India. It remained in the Far Eastern theatre throughout the 1939–45 war, primarily in the air defence role but also flying escort and ground attack sorties equipped with Hurricanes and Thunderbolts. The squadron was disbanded temporarily before reforming in Britain for a short spell as an anti-aircraft cooperation squadron. Then, in 1952 it began its long post war specialisation as an all weather

No longer just a Mae West . . . Tornado aircrew don their respirators and protective clothing prior to leaving the squadron operations block during a simulated chemical attack on RAF Leeming *(Author)*

fighter squadron: Vampire, Venom, Meteor,
Javelin, Lightning and finally the Tornado F3.

The other front line squadron which shares
Coningsby with 229 OCU and the Battle of
Britain Memorial Flight is No 29. 29 Squadron was formed at Gosport in November 1915,
two months after No 23, and in many respects
their subsequent histories have been similar. It
also moved to France in March 1916 equipped
with fighters and thereafter flew escort, interception and ground attack missions until
returning to the United Kingdom at the end of
the war to be temporarily disbanded.
Reformed in 1923, 29 Squadron continued its
day fighter role until it also converted to the
Blenheim 1F in December 1938. By 1 July
1940, it was declaring 10 aircraft serviceable
and five unserviceable at its Lincolnshire base
of Digby. As with the single engined fighters,
squadron aircraft 'establishment' was usually
16. Seldom was any squadron ever fully equipped, and virtually never were all aircraft
serviceable at one time. The day fighter
squadrons usually maintained an aircraft serviceability rate of between 66 and 75 per cent,
but the figures do not give a reliable indication
of ground crew effectiveness because of the
steady influx of new aircraft to replace battle
casualties. The Blenheims however were not
committed to the same extent to the battle, did
not suffer similar casualties and the steady
improvement in both aircraft systems reliability
and ground crew expertise can be seen in
increase in serviceability rates across the night
fighter squadrons during the Battle from less
than 60 to over 70 per cent. In 1990, serviceability rates for the Tornado and Phantom
force are classified, but it may be confidently
assumed that the squadron commanders
would not be happy with less than 75 per cent
daily availability.

Two actions by aircraft of 29 Squadron in
1940 illustrate both continuity of hazard and
change in operations, since that date. Sporadic
German raids took place during the night of 30
June, and Blenheims from 29 Squadron were
scrambled against them. One, flown by Pilot
Officer Susman, was seen to be 'fixed' by a
cone of searchlights which, it seems, had
mistaken him for a Ju 88. Apparently disorien-
tated by the blinding glare, he lost control and
crashed into the Lincolnshire countryside.

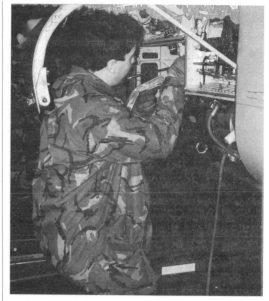

Junior Technician Steve Hughes changing the
Mauser gun on a No 29 Squadron F3 *(Author)*

Close as the personal relationship was between
Air Marshal Dowding and General Pile, there
was no experience in Britain, or anywhere else
for that matter, of tightly coordinated air-to-air
and surface-to-air defences. Anti-aircraft gun
crews were not accustomed to having friendly
aircraft in the skies at night, and in an age
before the radar was harnessed to Anti-
Aircraft (AA) guns there was no way an IFF
signal could be received. In 1990, with the
deployment of highly sophisticated surface to
air missile systems, the hazards of ground-to-
air 'Blue on Blue' remain, but are reduced by a
variety of organisational, tactical and technological means as explained in Chapter Six.

Later in the Battle, during a clear moonlit
night, a 29 Squadron Blenheim flying from the
satellite field at Ternhill in Shropshire was
directed by ground control towards an
intruder, which was visually identified as a
Heinkel III, south-west of Chester. Pilot
Officer R A Rhodes chased the Heinkel across
central and northern England for two hours
before he caught it 25 miles out over the North
Sea as it turned south-eastwards towards the
home base. All six members of the crew were
killed as it came down in the sea off the Norfolk
coast. The maximum speed of the Heinkel was
250 mph, that of the Blenheim 285 mph. That
the Heinkel was able to evade the Blenheim for

two hours may well have been due to the fact that its pilot was the highly experienced *Gruppenkommander* of 11 *Gruppe* of *Kampfgeschwader* 53, who managed to keep his aircraft out of Pilot Officer Susman's gunsights until, whether running short of fuel or finally making a tactical error by turning south towards his home base at Little Nord in Belgium, he was shot down.

Such an engagement would be highly unlikely in 1990. An intruder would be vulnerable to both kinds of missile carried by the Tornado or Phantom, regardless of either speed differential or skilful evasive flying, once the interceptor had closed to a distance which allowed visual identification, if indeed such closing had been necessary in the first place. Moreover, whereas in the Battle of Britain the Spitfires and Hurricanes flew by day, and the Blenheims largely by night, there would be no such distinction in 1990. The night/all-weather capabilities of the Tornadoes of No 29 Squadron would commit them to 24 hour operations, and the darkest of nights would offer no sanctuary to the intruders.

The Wattisham Wing

Two F4 Phantom squadrons remain in 11 Group service, Nos 56 and 74 at Wattisham. 56 was formed at Gosport in June 1916, moving to France for combat patrol and ground attack duties in the following April. It had early experience in United Kingdom air defence when it returned to Britain for two weeks in June 1917, together with 66 Squadron, to combat the daylight bombing threat to London. Only one raid was made in the period against Felixstowe and Harwich, far to the north of 56 Squadron's airfield at Petersbourne in Kent and no contact was made by the fighters. Ironically, two days after the return of the Squadron to France at the urgent request of Major General Trenchard, then commanding the RFC in France, 22 Gothas again attacked London in daylight, contributing to the decision of the British Government to investigate the state of the air war effort and organisation.

In common with many other squadrons, 56 was disbanded after the war and reformed at Hawkinge in 1922 to assume the fighter role it has discharged ever since. In May 1938 it became the second squadron to receive the Hurricane Mark I. Some detached flights from the squadron operated from French airfields during the Battle for France and flew defensive patrols over Dunkirk. Its permanent base, however, throughout the Battle of Britain, was North Weald. On 1 July 1940, the squadron reported 16 aircraft out of 18 ready for combat. Its first confirmed kill was achieved three days later with the destruction of a Dornier 17 off the coast near Burnham. For two months, the squadron fought every day, at first defending Channel convoys and then committed to defence of the airfields of south-east England. On 1 September, the squadron reported nine serviceable aircraft out of 14, but those figures concealed the loss of 11 aircraft in the previous five days alone. One pilot was killed, four wounded and the other six able to return to the battle, but the accumulated impact was such that the Commander-in-Chief withdrew 56 to regroup at Boscombe Down. Since 1 July, Fighter Command had lost 11 out of 46 squadron commanders, and 39 out of 97 flight commanders. The impact on experience levels and leadership was becoming acute, and replacements were arriving with only 20 hours' experience on type and with little or no simulated combat training. Many pilots died on their first sortie before receiving any instructions on the deadly art of the dogfight.

The respite afforded 56 Squadron did not last long as it was called into the crucial battles over south-east England just 10 days after deploying to Boscombe Down. Subsequently it flew Typhoons, Spitfires and Tempests before re-equipping in 1946 with Meteors in the peacetime defence of the United Kingdom. Since then, with the exception of a spell in Cyprus, the squadron has remained in 11 Group, flying Phantom FGR2s from Wattisham since 1976.

No 74, the second at Wattisham, is also equipped with the Phantom, but a different mark, the F4J, acquired from the US Navy in 1974, originally as a stop gap pending the arrival in service of the Tornado F3. The squadron was formed at Northolt in July 1917 and flew combat patrols and ground attack sorties in France until the Armistice. Unusually for a famous squadron, it was then

Phantom F4J of No 74 Squadron *(Flt Lt Tony Dixon)*

disbanded for 16 years, reforming in 1935 and moving anonymously to Malta as a precautionary move during the Abyssinian crisis. After six months it returned to Britain and began its long association with United Kingdom air defence at Hornchurch. In February 1939, 74 Squadron became the third RAF squadron to equip with Spitfires, forming an all-Spitfire Hornchurch wing with 75 and 65. On 1 July, it declared 10 out of 17 serviceable. Two days later, among all the individual personal tragedies which were occurring in the skies above south-east England, surely the most bizarre was the loss of Sergeant White when his Spitfire was struck by lightning near Margate. The modern interceptor may occasionally receive a jolt while flying through a heavy electric storm, but modern technology ensures that the fate of Sergeant White is unlikely to be repeated.

Throughout July, 74 Squadron flew from the forward operating base at Manston. Often the pilots were flying three or four sorties a day; indeed, on Sunday 11 August most had been in combat three times before lunch. During the six weeks, one of the most famous fighter leaders in the Battle, A G (Sailor) Malan was promoted from flight to squadron commander and personally accounted for six German aircraft, three of them after the squadron was pulled back to Wittering on 14 August to 'refresh' after the incessant combat.

As these brief sketches have illustrated, 74 Squadron was not alone in flying repeated sorties day after day for several weeks. Every scramble was prompted either by the presence or the imminence of hostile aircraft. Every flight could produce combat, usually against opponents who were numerically superior and frequently more experienced. The primary targets were the Dornier, Heinkel and Junkers bomber squadrons which, although lacking the manoeuvrability of the escorting ME 109s, could and did give a very good defensive account of themselves. Many Spitfires and Hurricanes fell to the guns of crews who already had many hours combat experience over European skies: German pilots such as Werner Molders, who came off second best in a tussle with "Sailor" Malan, Walter Rubensdorffer, who was killed on 15 August, Joachim Muncheberg, who had claimed 20 victories by 20 September, Helmut Wick with fifty-six. Adolf Galland and Hannes Trautloft, who both survived the war to become senior and respected Luftwaffe generals, matched in professional skills and individual bravery the legendary Bader, Stanford Tuck, Lacey, Finucane, Malan, Deere and the rest of the defending pilots. Skill could be measured by the number of kills achieved, and indeed the number of sorties survived. Bravery however usually went unrecorded, and sometimes not even witnessed, by friends.

The cumulative impact of combat fatigue and psychological stress in the face of overwhelming odds day after day took its toll on all the squadrons, and the skill of Air Marshal Dowding in rotating them from the front line at various stages of the Battle was undoubtedly a factor in sustaining his forces through the duration of the eight critical weeks between July and mid-September. His own personal experience, when, as a squadron commander in France in the first World War, he had seen at first hand the impact of sustained combat and heavy losses on a relatively small number of men, gave him the vision and judgement to extract his squadrons from the front line in 1940 before they reached breaking point.

No 8 Squadron in formation *(Flt Lt Kim Coxon)*

Combat Air Patrol: Soviet style SU27 Flanker B with full weapon load over the Baltic
(Swedish Air Force via Flygrapennytt)

The Succession: Tornado F3 and Spitfire Mk IIA over Lincolnshire in 1989 *(Sgt Rick Brewell ABiPP)*

Hawk varieties over the Welsh coast *(RAF Brawdy)*

Rapier firing on Benbecula Range *(British Aerospace)*

Phantom FGR2 of No 56 Squadron over the Akrotiri Peninsula in Cyprus *(Sgt Rick Brewell ABiPP)*

HAS preparation: No 23 Squadron Tornado on routine turn round *(Sqn Ldr T R Paxton)*

Dressed for the hunt: Tornado of No 23 Squadron carrying a QRA weapon load *(Sqn Ldr T R Paxton)*

Getting ready for Sentry: a NATO multi-national AWACS E3 is inspected by a Tornado
(Sqn Ldr T R Paxton)

Goodwill Migs. Mig 29s en route to Farnborough *(Sqn Ldr T R Paxton)*

F3 from 11 Sqn refuelling from No 216 Squadron TRISTAR *(Sqn Ldr T R Paxton)*

Topping up between practice intercepts: two Tornadoes of No 5 Squadron prodding with a Victor of No 55 Squadron *(Sqn Ldr T R Paxton)*

F3 of No 5 Squadron carrying long range fuel tanks *(Sqn Ldr T R Paxton)*

Tornado reheated: swept wing acceleration *(Flt Lt Ian Black)*

TU 142 Bears being escorted out of Iceland's air defence region by a USAF F15 Eagle of No 57 Fighter Interceptor Squadron *(USAF)*

Tornado of No 11 Squadron with long range tanks *(Flt Lt Ian Black)*

Chapter Four

SQUADRON LEADERSHIP

I N 1990, THE circumstances are very different. The determination of successive British governments to ensure that the country would never again face such a crisis so unprepared as the RAF was in 1940 has produced a fighting force equipped and trained to meet an opponent literally at a few minutes notice. The Soviet Union has, over the last 20 years, given priority to the creation of an air force prepared to carry out its strategy of a large scale air offensive at the outset of any conflict with the West. If such an attack were ever to be mounted, it would be met by aircrew who lacked combat experience, as indeed would their opponents. Combat training, begun at Brawdy, Chivenor and the two OCUS, is progressively honed, day by day, in flying which resembles, as closely as is possible in peacetime, their potential combat operations.

As in 1940, the example and professional skill of the squadron commander is paramount. All the Tornado and Phantom squadron commanders have many hundreds of hours experience in their air defence role, and most on the actual type of aircraft flown by their squadron. Wing Commander Graham Clarke for example, who has inherited command of 74 Squadron has a total of 3,500 flying hours, 850 of which are on the Phantom, and 2,500 on the Lightning. In addition, he has completed staff tours dealing with air-to-air missile procurement tactics and trials and has completed the RAF Staff College Course. In conversation with the author, he explained the responsibilities and activities of a modern fighter squadron commander.

He is responsible for ensuring that his squadron is prepared at any time to meet the aircraft generation rates demanded by AOC 11 Group, usually defined in percentages available for instant response, with further proportions ready for take off in periods measured in minutes and a very small number of hours. His Flight Commanders are responsible for constructing the day-to-day peacetime flying programmes, in accordance with the guidelines laid down for the Group by AVM Wratten's staff which indicate the number and types of sorties to be flown by all squadrons. There is a steady flow of new, 'ab initio' aircrew into the squadron, and Wing Commander Clarke must ensure that their needs, to be brought to combat readiness, are balanced with the requirement that his experienced crews remain current. He is one of the pilots in the squadron competent to lead formations of eight aircraft, although the bulk of the operational training concentrates on flights involving pairs or fours. He leads sorties himself or will fly as No 2 to a less experienced pilot, thereby observing developing proficiency from the air. As a result, the squadron commander flies at least as many hours as any squadron pilot, and frequently more. Indeed, on the morning of his conversation, Wing Commander Clarke had just stood down from a period of 24 hours standby as one of the 'Quick Reaction Alert' (QRA) crews who are always close to cockpit readiness in a proportion of the United Kingdom squadron aircraft.

In 1940, the fighter crews were scrambled by radio telephone from huts close to their parked aircraft, running across the grass clad in a variety of clothing: some in short sleeves, some in battle dress, some in their best blue uniforms clutching helmets and gloves and donning Mae West life jackets as they ran. In 1990, each aircraft, or pair of aircraft, would move out from their hardened shelter (HAS) and visual contact between squadron commander and his colleagues would be restricted to the other aircraft alongside. The CO would be likely to lead a pair, not the kind of formation led by Douglas Bader, John Thompson or 'Sailor' Malan. With the fighters dispersed around the airfield in HAS, communications are even more important. Individual choice of clothing

has long been abandoned. The modern fighter pilot waits on standby in a small room close to his aircraft dressed in a 'G' suit which automatically controls by pressure the circulation of blood round his body when the aircraft is manoeuvring under high G force, covered by his flying overall, an immersion suit and life jacket which would protect him if he were to eject from his aircraft while over the sea. Records of losses over the Channel in 1940 include a distressing number of pilots who baled out successfully but who then succumbed in the water either from hypothermia

Below: Uninterrupted Detachment: Tornadoes of No 23 Squadron on detachment to Akrotiri *(SACW Julie-Ann Timbrell)*
Left: Tornado of No 25 Squadron being drawn out of its HAS at Leeming *(Author)*

or drowning. Modern survival kit has on many occasions saved the lives of aircrew who in earlier generations could not have endured the water temperatures of the North Sea.

Wing Commander Clarke described two training exercises which play an important part in developing the skills of the squadron pilot. The first, 'Red Flag', takes place over the Nevada desert in the United States, where representative targets have been constructed on the ground, protected by replicas of Soviet air defence systems. Fighters participating in the exercises take it in turns to defend the target areas and then switch roles to acting as escorts for attacking formations. No ammunition is used, but all the ensuing simulated air-to-air combat is recorded by a very sophisticated set of cameras and electronic systems, so that back on the ground, the aircrew can subsequently examine and evaluate their individual performances. For example, a 30 aircraft 'raid' could be escorted or preceded by fighters to sweep the combat air patrols flying in wait for the bombers. The defending fighters, on the other hand, exactly like the Spitfires and Hurricanes, would be required to break up the bomber formations before they could drop bombs or launch their air-to-surface missiles, while at the same time either evading or engaging the attacking fighter screen. Except for flight safety considerations, there are no limits to the combat: high, medium and low level up to supersonic speeds, and all in a dense electronic warfare environment. Not surprisingly, Wing Commander Clarke shares the view of all his air defence colleagues that 'Red Flag' is the most valuable and realistic of all exercises undertaken by the squadrons. He could be flying with or against USAF 'aggressor' squadrons equipped with F16s but flown like Migs, with F111s, EF111s, Jaguar, Tornadoes and F15s from many different countries, supported as appropriate by inflight refuelling. Had such training been available for the RAF squadrons of 1939, the cost in lives of fighter pilots would assuredly have been greatly reduced in the Battle of Britain.

A second, smaller scale form of combat training takes place periodically at Decimomanu, a NATO base run by the Italian Air Force in Sardinia. Similar monitoring systems

to those in Nevada record the progress of individual combat with simulated missile firing. For two–three weeks the entire squadron can concentrate on perfecting combat skills in an environment particularly beneficial to the less experienced aircrew. In both exercises the aircrew have to develop tactical expertise which can enable them to operate against opponents whose aircraft may posses some technological advantage: exactly the situation of the Hurricane pilot when faced by the ME109.

Although well supported by his subordinates the squadron commander has extensive responsibilities on the ground as commander of 130 airmen and aircrew. 'Talent spotting' – the identification and grooming of aircrew to accept progressively more demanding responsibilities is a major task. Of particular importance is the identification of men with the potential to be Qualified Weapon Instructors (QWI). They must not only be highly competent but have the spare capacity to develop tactical awareness in the air and to be able to recall, analyse, debrief and train their junior colleagues on the ground. Usually, the potential QWI will be near the end of his first tour of duty with 4–500 hours on type. He will already

Junior Technician Kol Gavin removing engine module plates on a Tornado of No 5 Squadron *(Author)*

have demonstrated his skills as a pairs or fourship leader after a short supplementary course given on the squadron. One major change from 1940, and a reflection of the combined teamwork required on both the Tornado and the Phantom, is that the QWI may be either a pilot or a navigator.

A fundamental responsibility of the squadron commander is the maintenance of morale among his men and women. Supervision of the ground crew devolves through the squadron senior and junior engineer officers, but in the last resort it is the leadership and example of the squadron commander which will pervade the whole. 74 Squadron, in common with sister squadrons, has to spend time on detachments away from base, for gunnery training in Cyprus, for combat training in Sardinia, for participation in 'Red Flag' exercises and for equally important but less exotic visits to bases closer to air-to-air ranges in the United Kingdom. In addition, crews from 74 and 56 squadrons rotate on detachment to No 1435 Flight defending the Falkland Islands. Effective peacetime air defence, although not generating the combat stress of 1940, regularly demands long hours, absences from home and accumulated fatigue whose impact on the squadron members has to be carefully monitored and, wherever possible, alleviated by the squadron commander.

He will know all his men personally, and his aircrew especially well. Each year Wing Commander Clarke will write a confidential report on all his officers which will assess their performance in their duties, their personal attributes and their potential for promotion. The comprehension and accuracy of those reports is essential to ensure that promotion boards at the RAF Personnel Management Centre in Gloucester are able to make the best possible selection of future RAF squadron commanders. Hopefully, they will be required in a natural peacetime rotation. In war, many more could be required, as in 1940, in a very short space of time.

The Qualified Weapons Instructor

Within the fighter squadron, the role of the QWI is fundamental to the honing of the aircrew's combat skills. In 1940 there was no such appointment; even had there been he would have had no opportunity to exercise his influence, except on rare occasions in the front line after 7 September, when the Luftwaffe relaxed its offensive against Fighter Command on switching to attacks against London, or on the occasions when squadrons were extracted to recoup their strength. At that point one could argue, it was too late to develop combat skills.

Squadron Leader John Middleton is a navigator, and QWI on No 5 Squadron with the Coningsby Wing. He has flown with air defence squadrons for eight years, punctuating tours on the Phantom and F3 with a spell on Tornado GR1s. Since his entrance to the RAF as a Cranwell cadet he has amassed a total of 3,400 flying hours, including 550 on the F3. Again the contrast with 1940 is stark. Even those pilots who brought previous squadron experience to their task in July 1940 had not been prepared for the kind of combat they were to face. They evolved their combat tactics in the bloody school of experience, if they survived long enough at the hands of Molders, Wick and the rest.

Squadron Leader Middleton described the comprehensive combat training given to squadron aircrew once they arrive on a Tornado squadron from the OCU across the airfield at Coningsby. There are always two kinds of aircrew in a squadron, some 'ab initio' and others with previous air defence experience. It is the responsibility of the RAF Personnel Management Centre to provide a balance in each squadron in proportions of 'ab initio' and experience agreed with the chain of command. The QWI's responsibility is to take the crews through the squadron conversion syllabus up to combat readiness. He gives in-depth briefings on weapon systems, some sorties he will lead himself and in others he participates, analyses and debriefs. Each kind of missile has firing parameters and the aircrews' objective is to place the fighter in the right place at the right time to be within those firing parameters. They are recorded by on board systems for subsequent post sortie analysis to determine whether the intercept was carried out effectively.

Squadron Leader Middleton emphasised the need for aggression, technical expertise, combat awareness and flexibility of response to rapidly changing circumstances. Different operational skills are required from pilot and navigator but general attributes are similar, and both must function as a close-knit team. In the early stages, sorties are not too heavily loaded, with an experienced pilot flying with an 'ab initio' back-seater and vice versa. Progress is measured first by the experienced crew member, and then, when sufficient proficiency has been reached to permit the crewing of junior pilot with junior navigator, from another aircraft, all the time followed by post flight analysis of the on-board video and audio recorders. There are two critical points in progress, first when the crew are given a check ride before reaching limited combat readiness and then, later, the ability to close to a target at night with its lights out to make a visual identification check. Finally, at the end of some four months, comes a tactical check on the crew's ability to organise, brief, lead and debrief a simulated wartime sortie. In other words, the time taken in 1990 to bring a pilot to combat readiness, even after the exacting training given before he reaches his squadron, coincides almost exactly with the entire duration of the Battle of Britain from July to October 1940.

As Squadron Leader Middleton explained the pitfalls awaiting the novice fighter crews, the achievements of their relatively untrained predecessors became even more impressive. The novice will have difficulty in securing a missile firing position. His judgement of intercept angles, anticipation of enemy reaction and tactical awareness will all need to be developed. When he secures an attacking position, he may well pull the trigger before the associated safety switches are set, and air-to-air gunnery, still a fundamental fighter skill in the missile age, 'is all about tracking a target with a pipper', 'You can teach the principles but finally it is skill and experience which counts.' That statement says it all, about air-to-air combat in 1940 and combat in 1990. Not surprisingly the fighter pilot, and now the fighter navigator, require sharpness of eye, speed of reflex action, the cunning of a hunter and the aggression of a man who knows that on initiative may depend his survival.

Once the aircrew become combat ready,

they will participate in set exercises throughout the year. Training objectives will be met by sorties arranged with the EW Canberras from 360 Squadron at Wyton, low level engagements with Tornado GR1s and Jaguars and exercises with allied air forces, such as the F16s of the Royal Dutch Air Force. Missiles are fired on the range off the west of Scotland against Jindivik drones equipped with flares or radar enhanced targets as well as high speed targets launched by Canberras of 100 Squadron. The squadron will move to Cyprus each year, in flight refuelling en route, and then reach NATO gunnery standards against the Canberras' towed target banner, progressively acquiring accuracy with minimum passes in a minimum time. The fully operational crew will be skilled in the use of all three weapon systems: the beyond-visual-range radar guided Skyflash, the short range Sidewinder and the Mauser cannon.

The Flight Commander

All the senior officers of a squadron work together as a team and a key role is played by the flight commander: the man who since 1940 has been the closest to the squadron pilots and navigators.

Conversion from biplane to the fast monoplane Spitfire and Hurricane, or progression from flying training to front line squadron then frequently took place while the pilot was at the same time fighting to survive in the Battle itself. In early 1990, 43 Squadron was in the process of converting from Phantom to Tornado and Squadron Leader Jim Davidson, one of the flight commanders, explained the way in which the 'ab initios' from the flying schools were welded into a fighting unit alongside those who were familiar with the air defence task, but had to become proficient on a much more advanced fighter, and the sprinkling of crews bringing experience from existing F3 squadrons.

Squadron Leader Davidson has 2,400 flying hours, of which 1,500 have been amassed on the Tornado. He is a qualified flying instructor with experience on Jet Provosts, Hawks, Phantoms and Tornado GR1 as well as the F3 and so is well qualified to understand the challenge faced by both the air defence tyro and the old hand transferring to a new aircraft. At the time

of the conversion to the F3, his aircrews' experience ranged from 0 to 1,000 hours on type. In the recent past there had not been a major step from one aircraft to another, but now the advanced radar and weapon systems of the F3, for example the track-while-scan target acquisition, add a new dimension to interception and call for the mastery of new techniques. As a result the move to full combat readiness takes approximately the same time for both 'ab initios' and 'retreads', about four months to become operationally qualified as the junior crew in a pair.

The Leuchars wing could be expected to mount Combat Air Patrols (CAP) out to and beyond 600 miles, spending with inflight refuelling six hours or more on CAP. Although the presence of escort fighters cannot be discounted, the major task would be to destroy attacking bombers beyond-visual-range (BVR) with the radar guided Skyflash missile. As a result, the major concentration of operational work-up is on the combined tactics of a pair of F3s. Two basic types of attack are practised. The first, known as the 'bracket' involves the fighters approaching the incoming formation at a slant angle, one from each side, to secure a Skyflash firing position. The second, known as 'single side', keeps both fighters on the same side of the approaching bombers' track but their objective to make a successful BVR missile launch, remains the same. At closer range, the heat seeking AIM 9L Sidewinder would be used.

The F3 is not designed to be a highly manoeuvrable fighter in the tradition of the

Top: Phantom FGR2 of No 56 Squadron firing its Gatling gun on the gunnery range off Cyprus *(Sgt Rick Brewell)*

Above: Air-to-air missiles en route to the squadrons at RAF Leeming *(Author)*

Spitfire, but rather a long range destroyer. The aircrew, unlike their predecessors, would not deliberately seek out a close encounter unless no other option was available. Then, and especially at low level, where the Tornado's variable geometry wing would greatly enhance manoeuvrability, gunnery skills would be very important. As in 1990, incoming bombers could be heavily armed, with radar guided guns or even self defence air-to-air missiles, and so the Tornado crews must learn not just how to kill but how to survive.

The Squadron Instrument Rating Officer

On every squadron, one highly experienced officer will carry the responsibilities for developing basic flying competence. He will work closely with the squadron executives and may be known colloquially as the Squadron IRE – Instrument Rating Examiner – or QFI, the Qualified Flying Instructor or simply as Squadron Training Officer (STO).

The STO on 56 Squadron is Squadron Leader Jack Dowling, who has amassed a total of 4,400 hours, 2,500 of those on the Phantom. In addition to previous front line squadron tours, spells as a flying instructor at the Central Flying School and Chief Standards and Evaluation officer of the Phantom OCU have prepared him well for his duties on 56 Squadron. He outlined his responsibilites to the author.

'Ab initio' crews arrive in the squadron with a 'White Card' instrument rating which places restrictions, for example cloudbase and visibility, on the occasions when they can fly. As their proficiency increases, observed by both STO and other squadron executives, they will be checked for an instrument rating upgrade to 'Green', which may be awarded on a provisional basis allowing them to contribute to the task, or permanent, which will raise the height and weather limits on which they are assessed as competent to fly.

That level of competence would be determined by Squadron Leader Dowling himself, flying a 'check ride' in the back seat of the F4. In such a flight the white rated pilot would deal with simulated engine failures and demonstrate his airmanship in all aspects of air intercept sorties: precise speeds, rates of descent, angles of bank, hard 60° turns at 500 knots, disorientating deceleration and recovery on instruments and finally a return to base which depended on the use of ground radars and instruments in simulated – or real – bad weather. If successful, the pilot would be cleared to operate down to 200 feet in bad weather, and would have taken a major step to all-round operational competence.

The highest level is the Master Green rating, awarded after many more hours and much greater experience in airmanship after another check ride in which Green requirements are flown to the limits. Mere possession of the ratings is however insufficient: standards must be sustained, especially those of all the senior squadron executives, whose skills are checked annually by STOs, like Squadron Leader Dowling. As squadron QFI he checks a mixture of flying and instrument ability: general handling, aerobatics and particular situations such as high angle and attack manoeuvring, high nose low speed recovery, stalling and low flying. Specific air combat checks confirm a pilot's ability to handle his aircraft safely while concentrating primarily on his interceptions. Just to make sure that Squadron Leader Dowling's own standards don't drop he is checked annually by 'trappers' from the OCU who will also renew his instructor qualification.

In sum, the hard and frequently tragic lessons of 1940 have been taken to heart in today's front line squadrons. Combat is not the place to learn combat skills; combat skills demand finely tuned, almost instinctive, flying skills; both combat and flying skills need to be constantly practised and evaluated in as close to combat conditions as can be achieved in peacetime. Each senior member of a squadron has an individual contribution to make in a closely knit, highly effective team. That effectiveness is constantly measured in exercises, but there is in addition one regular activity which in many respects comes right to the threshold of a wartime situation: the discharge of the Quick Reaction Alert (QRA) task.

For many years during the period of confrontation with the Soviet Union a number of fighters, with their crews close by, have stood on various 11 Group airfields fully armed ready to scramble; to identify, challenge or, in case of

Operational turnaround under 'real' wartime conditions: Minival at Leeming *(Author)*

Friendly welcome: Tornado of No 5 Squadron escorts a Mig 29 towards Farnborough in 1988 *(Sqn Ldr T R Paxton)*

Bear Hunt: TU 95 with escorting Tornado from No 5 Squadron *(No 5 Squadron/Crown Copyright)*

surprise attack intercept, intruders into the United Kingdom Air Defence Region. In 1990, and until the hoped for international agreements on armed force reductions are in place, that task is sustained by Phantom and Tornado crews. Periodically, sometimes as often as three times a week, Russian long range aircraft approach, enter or en route to destinations in Cuba or West Africa, track across the Region. In November 1989 for example, Flight Lieutenant Ian McGregor of 11 Squadron was the Duty Force Commander at Leeming, as two Tornadoes waited in their HAS and four aircrew spent 24 hours fully kitted up a few yards away listening to the regular 'Beep, Beep' coming through the loudspeaker in their shelter which indicated that the line to Sector

Control was open for the transmission of a scramble message. Flight Lieutenant McGregor's precise responsibilities remain highly classified, but among them is to keep a regular check on weather states, not just at Leeming but out in the CAP area and at diversion airfields as far afield as Iceland and Norway, so that his crews are fully prepared for take off.

Two weeks earlier, the QRA task for the Leeming wing was being discharged by 23 Squadron, which had only recently completed conversion to the F3 and had not yet been scrambled. The Duty Force Commander, Flight Lieutenant Ian McDonald Webb was awakened from a fitful sleep on his bunk at 6 a.m. by a message that 'X Rays' – still the 11 Group tag for unidentified aircraft – had been spotted approaching the UKADR from around the North Cape of Norway. The tracks were not moving too quickly so with his navigator, Flight Lieutenant Mike Heaton, he had time to snatch a quick cup of coffee before the telebrief from Sector HQ at Buchan called them both to cockpit readiness. They ran the few yards to the waiting F3, the warning klaxon sounded and the HAS doors opened automatically. Strapped in, Flight Lieutenant McDonald Webb called 'cockpit ready' to Buchan and was immediately scrambled.

The F3 climbed away into the November dawn under local Leeming control and was given a direct track northwards, handed over to Scottish military radar at Prestwick, then to Wick and finally to the fighter controller on duty at Saxa Vord in the Shetlands where, coincidentally, the author was watching the air picture unfold on the radar screens. Meanwhile, a supporting tanker had been scrambled from Marham but Flight Lieutenant Heaton was busily engaged in the back seat working out diversion fuel calculations for Leuchars and Lossiemouth and the time available for the task should inflight refuelling not be available.

On the hand over to Saxa Vord, the controller checked the F3's endurance and gave up to date details on the unidentified tracks. Then, as usual, he gave the vector for the F3's CAP, but on this occasion followed it immediately with a direct course to steer to interception point. Normally the interceptor would head initially to the CAP nearest the projected intrusion point so that the unidentified aircraft could be given an 11 Group escort inside the UKADR.

Flight Lieutenant Heaton quickly made radar contact with the intruders. Then, while still some 40 miles away, the F3 crew saw the contrails of two aircraft, at 26,000 feet, one about eight miles behind the other, tracking down towards the United Kingdom. The size of the contrails suggested that they were being made by some variant of the Russian Tu 95 Bear. Flight Lieutenant McDonald Webb told Buchan he had radar contact, and double checked, with visual correlation that these were indeed the incoming 'X Rays', giving height and estimated speed.

The next decision was which Bear to intercept, and then which kind of approach. Flight Lieutenant McDonald Webb elected to intercept the second aircraft from an initial position 90 degrees to it, allowing the pair to cross the F3 about five miles ahead. He then swung the Tornado in behind the No 2. This peacetime approach was obviously quite different from a combat interception in war, when missiles would have been launched much earlier from a different angle. The Bears were now clearly recognisable as naval reconnaissance aircraft, and Flight Lieutenant McDonald Webb closed steadily until he was close enough to examine the shape of the intruder in detail and record it with the camera carried on board for that purpose. On this occasion the Russian crew were just as keenly interested in the F3, perhaps because this was the first time they had seen in close up a Tornado in 23 Squadron's colours. Their snapshots were taken by a massive camera in the rear turret. Separated by an appropriate flight safety margin the Tornado stayed with the Bear for several minutes until both Russian aircraft, their mission of probing the air defences complete, turned 180 degrees and headed north, perhaps to reach base in time for their equivalent of Happy Hour and a long weekend. En route, they were shepherded by F16s of the Norwegian Air Force. Meanwhile the Tornado had linked up with the friendly tanker from 55 Squadron and headed for home. On this occasion the meeting had been amicable; both sides had no doubt added to their countries' intelligence data and retained a few more photos for the squadron linebook. Two more Russian crews had learned that they had no chance of penetrating the UKADR without interception, and the tight teamwork between 11 Group's ground controller and aircrew had been proved one more time.

The successful interception by Flight Lieutenants McDonald Webb and Heaton was achieved by professional skill which typified all other aircrew in the front line squadrons. They would be the first to admit their dependence not just on the fighter controller at Saxa Vord but on the many thousands of men and women in 11 Group whose essential individual contributions on the ground ensured that they, and their aircraft were prepared to respond successfully at no notice to such demands.

Chapter Five

FLYING SUPPORT

I N 1940 THE Battle of Britain squadrons received indirect assistance from Bomber Command whose raids on targets in western Europe frequently diverted Luftwaffe fighters away from their primary concentration at the time of escorting their own bombers against Britain. And, indeed, in any future conflict it is unlikely that the government of the day would permit an opponent sanctuary on his own territory from which to mount uninterrupted operations against this country. The RAF's Tornado GR1 squadrons, for example, could be expected to take the war back to the opponent's own skies. In 1990, however, the fighter squadrons of 11 Group do not simply receive indirect support but rely very heavily on three kinds of complementary flying activity, some of it provided by aircraft from Nos 1 and 18 Groups.

The Wyton Canberra Wing

The Canberra squadrons at RAF Wyton, Nos 360 and 100 make a major contribution to the peacetime preparedness of the front line fighters. In previous Chapters frequent references have been made to Electronic Warfare (EW) as, since those early days of 1940, radio and radar have become integral features of early warning and air-to-air combat. At first the only way to deal with radar early warning stations was by destroying them. On 12 August 1940 coordinated attacks were made by the Luftwaffe on Dover, Rye, Pevensey and Ventnor Chain Home (CH) stations. Ventnor was heavily damaged and put out of action for three days. Despite the overlapping coverage of the CH stations the Germans were able to take advantage of the gaps and deliver very destructive attacks on two of the forward airfields, Hawkinge and Manston. Had the Luftwaffe had the strength to keep the radar coverage dislocated, the subsequent effectiveness of the defending Spitfires and Hurricanes would have been severely impaired.

In 1990, three links in the air defence chain are vulnerable to electronic counter measures (ECM): the early warning radar, the aircraft's AI radar and the communications which link all the elements together and provide the basis for command and control. It would be unrealistic for 11 Group's fighters and fighter controllers to train day by day using unimpeded radio channels and clear pictures on their radar screens. 360 Squadron's task is to make things as awkward, confusing and unintelligible as peacetime conditions will allow. Conversations with aircrew on 360 Squadron clearly indicate that they thoroughly enjoy their battle of wits and frequently complement their electronic technology with tactical and personal innovations: exactly as the Luftwaffe did in 1940 when, as we saw in Chapter I, it jammed the CH stations in early September and used the callsign 'Apena' of one of the Czechoslovak squadrons to recall its aircraft to base in the middle of a dogfight.

Unlike all the other squadrons contributing to British air defence in 1990, No 360 has only been in service for a relatively short time, forming at RAF Watton in 1966 with personnel drawn from both RAF and Royal Navy. The naval link is maintained by regular training exercises against naval radars and communica-

49

tions. Usually about 25 per cent of the squadron will wear dark blue uniforms but the squadron is operated along traditional RAF lines. It is equipped with English Electric Canberra T17 and T17As with slightly different avionics. Even now, EW is the most arcane subject and in a future conflict would be one area in which an opponent could achieve technological and tactical surprise. Exact details of the training procedures used by 360 therefore remain classified, but Squadron Leader Peter Robinson and his colleagues were able to give a clear indication of the squadron's wide ranging activities. Regular exercises are flown against the Type 84 and Type 85 radar of the Ground Control Interception (GCI) stations whose controllers must learn to cope with jamming which will distort their screens and possibly obscure IFF signals. There is a consistent technological contest between ECM, and both manual and automated counter measures (ECCM). Training programmes for the OCU and squadrons are laid down by Headquarters Strike Command,

as are sorties against Bloodhound, Rapier and Skyguard surface-to-air defences. While most exercises are pre-briefed in outline with participating units, the radar, AI or SAM operators will not necessarily know what kind of interference to expect.

Each Canberra carries two ALQ 167 modified jamming pods in the original bomb bay, one forward and one rear together with two E/F and one D band jammers. The whole equipment, including chaff pods carried at the wing tip, can disrupt a wide range of frequencies from ground surveillance to AI. Radar jamming is usually accomplished by flooding the operating frequency to such an extent that the radar screen will be virtually obliterated. It may be done electronically, or mechanically by laying clouds of chaff: metallic strips cut in

Below: Canberra T17A of No 360 Squadron prepares to get airborne at RAF Wyton *(RAF Wyton)* *Right:* Samples of metal and glass fibre strips dropped as 'Chaff' to decoy and confuse radar emissions; as used by No 360 Squadron *(RAF Wyton)*

specific lengths to interfere with various frequencies. Alternatively, spurious signals may be generated by the Canberra to confuse the screen's interpretation by the operator. Communications may be obliterated, as a radio station or a commercial radio may be rendered inaudible by atmospherics or by the proximity of another station with a much more powerful signal. On the other hand, the operator's own frequency may be used to insert nonsense syllables over a transmission or be subject to 'garbling' in other ways. 'Spoofing' could entail use of a carefully edited tape of a controller's own voice, played immediately before the controller could be expected to contact a fighter at a particular stage of the sorties. In peacetime, such activities are limited by consideration of flight safety. In war, an opponent would regard degradation of an opponent's flight safety as an operational bonus.

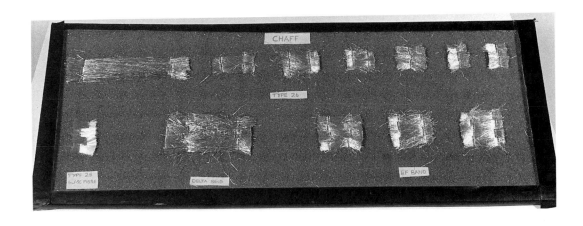

It is difficult to imagine the impact of such EW on aircrew in combat, when nerves are taut, when familiar voices should be reassuring, or when one is suddenly 'blinded' and deafened at a critical moment of an intercept. Certainly, embarrassment in peacetime is preferable to failure in combat. The object of No 360's activities is to make all operators aware of, and to be able to operate effectively in, electronic fog and uncertainty. Voiceless procedures, message authentication and autonomous operation must become virtually instinctive at a time when faculties are naturally seeking to concentrate on the physical threat, not the unseen electronic complication.

A complex training sortie was described by Squadron Leader Hugh Prior, one of 360's AEO Electrical Warfare officers, and Flight Lieutenant Eddy Craig who would in this case be the captain of the lead Canberra. The objective of the mission was to test the reaction of the radar controllers and fighters to a 'raid' simulating a number of aircraft protected by ECM. As usual, the Wyton crews, drawn from both 360 and 100 Squadrons would be given a preflight brief setting out the phases of the exercise, diversion airfields, radio frequency numbers and met conditions between Wyton and the exercise area. On the occasion briefed by Flight Lieutenant Craig, the weather state was a good example of the conditions regularly faced off the north-east coast of Scotland: a far cry from the cloudless skies enjoyed by crowds at RAF At Home Day displays or even the broken cloud of the daylight operations of 1940.

This was to be a night sortie, with a 2,000 foot cloud base in the operating area, with significant layers of cloud up to 20,000 feet. Between 3 and 8,000 feet there was the possibility of icing which can give a Canberra pilot problems not met by the aircrew of less venerable RAF aircraft. Although a well proven aircraft from an older and comparatively less sophisticated age, the Canberra can still present a challenge to young pilots who frequently graduate from it to Tornadoes and other fast jet combat aircraft. On every sortie the aircrew are given 'an emergency thought'. On this occasion it was fire in the air, not exactly what a young pilot recovering at night to Wyton in high cross winds, low cloud and heavy rain

would wish to encounter. In comments on 'routine' emergencies Flight Lieutenant Craig reminded the aircrew of hazards of bird strikes and pilot disorientation at night in bad weather. Overall, the briefing was a good illustration of what 'routine' can mean to all-weather crews.

Squadron Leader Prior described how the 360 Squadron Canberras would seek to mask the approach of their 'silent' partner, the target aircraft from 100 Squadron. As the T 17s climb away from Wyton, the Electronic Warfare Officer (EWO) prepares his jamming equipment. The major target is Buchan's Type 92 surveillance and early warning radar, which operates in the D band frequency of 1–2 Gigahertz (GHz) or 1–2,000 million cycles per second. AI radars are likely to transmit in the I band of 8–10 GHz and other jamming equipment is prepared for use against them. Then Squadron Leader Prior calls up Buchan to confirm that the 'raid' is on its way and the broad timing to expect radar and communications jamming. This is not the artificial scenario it may sound, because in war, the controller at Buchan would hope to receive early warning of the likelihood of hostile activity from other agencies among the allies on the continent or elsewhere, although not necessarily about the exact size and compositions of an incoming raid. Flight safety parameters are established – the preflight briefing has confirmed the absence of other aircraft in the area, but nothing is ever taken for granted. Meanwhile two F3s have taken off from Leuchars and the stage is set for the 'battle'.

Squadron Leader Prior checks that his tape recorder is set to contribute to spoofing and jamming of the fighter's voice communications and then begins to make life difficult for the Buchan controller. He identifies the Type 92 radar by such features as its aerial rotation period and pulse recurrence frequency. The position of all static British early warning radar is likely to be known to a potential opposition as, one assumes, are those of the potential opposition to friendly forces. The D band jammer is put across the Buchan transmission and stabilised. It is the fighter's turn next as the I band receiver searches for the AI signals and when they are identified, the technological and tactical battle of wits between F3 and T17 crews begins. The F3 crew must be able to respond to noise and modulated noise jamming, deception and distorted reflections of radar signals as well as spoof messages over the radio-telephone (R/T). Some will be countered by the F3's own ECCM technology, other will require quick-witted interpretation and counter by the crew themselves. This, in addition to flying the fighter safely and seeking to intercept both jammers and 'bombers'. All the while, below and behind the T17s, the 'Archer' Canberras from 100 Squadron stay silent with their simulated weapon loads of air-to-surface missiles.

At the appointed time, the Canberras turn for home, the F3s head for their East Fife base, and the Buchan controllers take time out for a coffee. The exercise will subsequently be analysed in detail by the squadrons, the controllers and the staffs. How effectively did the controller cope? Did the F3s find the Archer Canberras and 'destroy' them before missile launch point? What lessons have been learned? What new data needs to be passed down to Wing Commander Mal Gleave at the F3 OEU? What further unpleasant refinements can Squadron Leader Prior and his colleagues in 360 construct before their next combined exercise?

Sorties are also flown against the surface-to-air defences – Bloodhound, Rapier and Skyguard all rely on radar for some stage of their effectiveness. On these missions, the T17s usually represent aircraft with self-screening equipment rather than accompanying a silent partner. One tactic which can be employed against all radars which incorporate Doppler shift in their systems is a 'Zero Doppler' turn in the T17's low level attack run, thereby impairing the radar's ability to ascertain the target's velocity. Tactical evasion is also practised by the Canberra against the interceptors. Timely manoeuvre can upset the geometry of an interception accompanied, for example, by the scattering of chaff or by evading the AI beam. Meticulous timing and precision flying are both required for such evasion, because if the Canberra out-turns the limits of its own screening, the F3 would be presented with a very easy target. Not surprisingly, the crews of 360 Squadron exude a confident professionalism which reflects their unique and essential contribution to the training of their colleagues in the air and on the ground in 11 Group.

The two silent 'Archer' members of Squadron Leader Prior's exercise against the Northern Sector air defences were drawn from 360's partner squadron at Wyton, No 100. Commanded by Wing Commander Keith Douglas, No 100 is also part of 18 Group but 80 per cent of its flying and three of its major roles, providing Silent Targets, Target Towing and Chaff Laying, support 11 Group Operations. After its formation in 1917, the squadron had a distinguished night bombing record in the First World War and flew on operations in Europe and the Far East throughout the

Combined services to confuse: Corporal Peter Hylton (RAF) and Leading Air Engineer Stuart Laurie (RN) loading the wingtip chaff canister on a Canberra T17A of No 360 Squadron (*Author*)

Above: An 'Archer' Canberra of No 100 Squadron
(Flt Lt Kim Coxon)
Right: A Rushton target under the wing of a
Canberra of No 100 Squadron. The six flares used
as targets for surface to air missile practice are
clearly visible *(RAF Wyton/Crown Copyright)*

Second. Legend asserts that the skull and
crossbones motif on the squadron badge was
acquired from a French house of questionable
repute in 1918, but the precise circumstances
remain unclear. The Malayan squadron motto,
'Never stir up a hornet's nest' on the other
hand was earned in combat against the Japan-
nese in 1942. Thereafter, the squadron flew
Lancasters throughout the Bomber Offensive
against Germany and in 1954 first equipped
with the English Electric B2 Canberra. A spell
of seven years flying Victor II V bombers at
Wittering was followed after a short break with
its assumption in 1972 of its current responsibilities. Ten years later, the squadron moved to
Wyton, absorbing aircraft, aircrew and
groundcrew from Nos 7 and 13 Squadrons. In
the 'Silent Target' role 100 contributes to
many aspects of 11 Group preparedness. It
provides practice interception targets for the
School of Fighter Control at Boulmer, for
Sector Operations Centres, and AEW aircraft.
It flies frequently in low level four aircraft
formation as targets for the various stages of F3
and F4 crew combat training and low level
sorties against the Bloodhound, Rapier and
Skyguard operators. Finally, it participates
weekly in large scale exercises against combined 11 Group defences.

It is in short far more than just a target
towing squadron, although these sorties, involving either a Rushton target over the Hebrides
range or a 'banner' from the Armament
Practice camps at Akrotiri, provide the fighter
crews with essential live firing opportunities.
The Rushton target is deployed by a winch at
the end of 20,000 feet of wire cable and
simulates both radar reflection and infra red
emissions. Each of two targets offer six firing
opportunities to the missile operators. The
gunnery banner measures 30 feet by 6 feet,
towed 900 feet behind the Canberra. With the
advent of the F3 and its highly effective
Mauser cannon, consumption of banners has
increased dramatically and the number of

sorties required to reach NATO standards have dropped.

Chaff laying remains a 360 Squadron responsibility, but without having to carry ECM equipment in bomb bays, the long range ex-photographic reconnaissance PR 7s now contribute to this activity also, using chaff-dispenser hoppers mounted in modified wing-tip tanks.

Flight Lieutenant Andy Fillingham, one of the 100 Squadron navigators, described in more detail how the B2s worked first with the trainee crews on 229 OCU at Coningsby, and then with the front line squadrons. In the OCU Basic Radar phase of training, two Canberras would meet up with the F3 at about 17,000 feet off the coast over the North Sea. They would represent different kinds of attack, flying spread out in a wide battle formation, or in echelon, or as bombers with a fighter escort or in trail one behind the other. The fighter crew would not know beforehand which one, or combination, to expect. On hearing the call 'Judy' from the F3 crew, indicating that the targets had been picked up and the F3 was going to autonomous AI, the Canberras would prepare for evasive action. The rate of evasion would depend on the OCU training level reached and would progressively increase to complicate the work load of the F3 crew. Sometimes, by previous agreement with the OCU staff pilot, evasion would begin before Judy was called so that the trainee navigator could see on his screen what an evasive turn looked like.

Subsequently, when the crews are working up to combat readiness on the squadrons, the Canberras will provide much more complicated target patterns. They would include low level penetrations at 250 feet against CAPs 6,000 feet above them or 'bat and ball' exercises with two F3s working from opposite ends of a racetrack pattern, or high level intercepts at 45,000 feet, when the F3 would practise climbing, missile firing intercepts. Flight Lieutenant Fillingham confirmed the impression given by his colleagues across on 360 Squadron, that while they derived great satisfaction from seeing the progressive development of the fighter crew, from novice to accomplished all-weather hunter, they relished the tactical difficulties which their relatively elderly aircraft could present while that level of competence was being achieved.

In 1990 it was a subject for continuous, good humoured inter-squadron banter, fostered by frequent joint detachments and inter-unit visits. In 1940 there was no simulated enemy; no banter; and inter-unit visits tended to be permanent.

In-Flight Refuelling

In 1940 the ME 109 pilots had to keep a sharp eye on their fuel gauges, using rules of thumb to work out the gallons needed to return to base in northern France. Miscalculation would put them into the Channel or, if over-cautious, pull them out of combat before their fuel state justified it. It was not just a question of a hypothetical combat radius on unopposed escort or fighter sweep, but how rapidly a full throttle, sweetened by direct fuel injection into the Daimler Benz 12 cylinder engine would drain the tanks in a cartwheeling dogfight. Recurring again and again in Luftwaffe aircraft loss reports are expressions like 'Engine failure not due to combat . . .' or 'crash landed without previous combat damage . . .' Not all were caused by running out of fuel; but what would have been the impact on the Battle of a squadron of German in-flight refuelling aircraft orbiting with impunity over the Pas de Calais, able to top up the Messerchmitts either to extend their endurance, get them back to base, or even more significantly, to allow them to return immediately to the fray?

Conversely, suppose Air Vice Marshal Park's Spitfires and Hurricanes had been able to mount combat air patrols sustained by Royal Air Force in-flight refuelling. Gone would have been the fears of ground controllers of scrambling their squadrons too early. Refuelled at the top of their initial climb from their airfields, the British fighters could have picked their height and position to bounce the intruders. The 'Big Wing' controversy arose when Air Vice Marshal Leigh-Mallory wished to launch his 12 Group fighters from East Anglia en masse but Air Vice Marshal Park argued that such concentration unacceptably delayed Douglas Bader and his fellow squadron commanders joining the fray. Had the Coltishall Squadrons been able to refuel in-flight and join combat air patrols over the Thames estuary, far greater, timely concentrations could have taken place and a great deal of unfortunate recrimination would have been avoided.

In 1990, Air Vice Marshal Wratten does not face that problem. He can draw upon air-to-air, or in-flight, refuelling (AAR) for his interceptors from two specialist and one multi-role AAR squadrons under the day to day control of AOC 1 Group. The three squadrons: 55 at Marham, 101 and 216 at Brize Norton provide AAR for the whole of the Royal Air Force, of which in peacetime about 50 per cent is allocated to air defence related activities. Broad allocation of effort, and detailed planning of large scale tanker exercises are done at headquarters RAF Strike Command at High Wycombe, whose Commander-in-Chief has overall responsibility for all RAF operations in the United Kingdom other than basic and advanced flying training.

No 55 Squadron

The most senior of the tanker squadrons is No 55, based at Marham in Norfolk. 55 was formed in April 1916 at Castle Bromwich and after flying DH4s in France, moved after the war to the Middle East, where it remained until 1946, carrying out light bomber operations against Rommel's forces and supply lines in the Western Desert and accompanying Allied forces into Sicily in 1944. After post-war disbandment, the squadron reformed in 1960 at Honington with the third of the RAF's nuclear armed V bombers, the Victor B1/1A, which could also carry a 35,000 lb conventional bomb load. In 1965 it assumed its current refuelling role at Marham, re-equipping in 1975 with the Victor K2.

In 1990, 55 Squadron, under the command of Wing Commander David Williams is manned by 165 aircrew and groundcrew. Among its many responsibilities, it shares with the Brize Norton squadrons the task of maintaining aircraft at take off readiness 24 hours a day, 365 days a year, in support of the interceptor force QRA aircraft.

Flight Lieutenant Stephen McLaughlin is a tanker captain on 55 Squadron with a total of 2,100 flying hours, 1,300 of them on Victor tankers. He discussed with the author the kind of rapidly responsive sortie which last November supported Lieutenant McDonald Webb's 'Bear hunt' described in the last chapter. When Northern Sector Control Centre at Buchan received warning from NATO colleagues in Norway that X-Rays were heading towards the UKADR, the Victor crew was brought to an advanced readiness state. There would either be a pre-briefed flight profile, with updates on met, fuel requirements and contact frequencies, or the crew would be given an update once airborne. The actual 'Scramble' message, which would prompt the Victor crew to rush Battle-of-Britain-style across to their aircraft, could indicate the CAP position from which the fighter intercept would be mounted, or could simply give the Victor a course to steer.

Once airborne, the Victor could be joined by the interceptor, or it could rendezvous later. In November, the tanker did not meet up with Flight Lieutenant McDonald Webb until after the intruder identification had been made. As the Victor headed north, the captain contacted

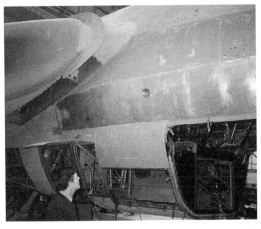

Squadron Leader Eric Sergeant examining the cockpit fuselage area of a Victor K2 undergoing major servicing at Marham in the Victor Maintenance Unit *(Author)*

Buchan and was given the current situation report and the rendezvous point with the F3. Frequency security was maintained by reference to predetermined numbers in a classified pad carried by all the participants in the scramble. The tanker captain established contact with the F3 and with the controlling ground station at Saxa Vord, to ensure that he was in position when the interceptor was ready to refuel.

In due course, Flight Lieutenants McDonald Webb and Heaton, well satisfied with 23 Squadrons first 'blood' announced their imminent arrival for a 'top up'. The Victor trailed the 80 feet of centre line hose and maintained its racetrack pattern within the equipment-designer speed limit of 320 knots. After a few minutes, the 23 Squadron F3 appeared beyond the Victor's port wing tip just far enough for the tanker captain to see him and exchange visual greetings. The presence of the trailing hose indicated that the tanker was ready for fuel transfer, known colloquially as 'prodding', to begin.

The tanker crew then carried out their regular procedures. The captain oversees and is in charge of the operation while maintaining constant height and speed and trying to avoid cloud and clear air turbulence. Once fuel transfer has begun, light cloud presents no problems, but for obvious reasons visual references are required for the prodding to take place. The co-pilot was monitoring the aircraft fuel state, computing how much the tanker could transfer and how much it would need itself to recover to base or diversion airfield. The navigator was keeping a sharp visual lookout to ensure that no other aircraft would present a flight safety hazard, while keeping track of the Tornado.

The F3 dropped back behind the tanker and the navigator began a running commentary on its approach to the 'basket' at the end of the hose. After a few seconds he reported that the F3 was astern and stabilised and the hose was free from oscillation. At that point the tanker captain would switch the pairs of lights on either side of the Hose and Drogue Unit at the rear of the fuselage from red to amber, indicating that the Victor was ready to receive a prod. Steadily, with a closing speed of 5–10 knots, the Tornado moved forward to slot its fuselage mounted probe into the drogue basket, aiming to compress the hose by at least 7 feet to ensure a lock-in. This delicate exercise takes place with the aircraft some 70 feet apart at 300 miles an hour. Smooth but firm contact will open the non-return valve and two green lights will indicate that the fuel is starting to flow. Meanwhile the Victor AEO will watch his intruments measuring the outtake at 4,000 lbs per minute. The fighter can breakaway at any time, automatically closing the valve, or the AEO can restrict the metered flow at a predetermined amount and when the fuel is stopped, the green lights would be replaced by amber. In the case of the 23 Squadron Tornado, Flight Lieutenant Heaton would have calculated the amount of fuel required to see them safely back to Leeming with sufficient to cover an emergency diversion. Had there been an emergency, the tanker captain, in sole command of the situation, would have instructed the F3 to break off or, if R/T communication had been lost, switched the green lights to red. Happily, on this as on most occasions, the prod was completed successfully, and both aircraft returned uneventfully to their bases. If R/T communication had been lost before prodding took place, a standard emergency procedure would have been followed. The fighter would have moved up alongside the tanker as normal. If the hose was not already trailing, the Victor captain would lower it to indicate that the fighter could begin the

Phantoms Tanking: An F4J from No 74 Squadron takes on fuel from a VC10K of No 101 Squadron while an F4GR2 from No 56 Squadron waits its turn *(RAF Wattisham/Crown Copyright)*

prodding sequence. If the hose was already out, he would switch his external anti-collision lights on and off to pass the same message. Thereafter the 'traffic lights' could be sufficient on their own to guide the silent F3 through the prod.

The Brize Norton Squadrons

On that particular day in November 1989, the QRA support task was met by a Victor of 55 Squadron, but on other days it could equally well have been one of the tankers from Brize Norton, who share the task equally with the Victors.

Brize Norton has never been a fighter base since its construction before the Second World War but during the Battle of Britain it had a thoroughly unwelcome experience at the hands of the Luftwaffe. On Friday 16 August, at the height of the Battle, two JU 88s reached Oxfordshire undetected in what is believed to have been a carefully planned raid, timed to avoid fighters likely to be back on the ground refuelling – an ironic detail in the light of Brize Norton's current responsibilities. Approaching at low level in the evening haze the two aircraft dropped 35 bombs on the hangars destroying 46 aircraft and damaging another 18, including 11 Hurricanes in the resident maintenance unit. The two Ju 88s escaped as skilfully as they had come, with no Ju 88 losses – or kills – being reported by either side that day.

In 1940 Brize Norton was not a vital target in the struggle for air supremacy over south-east England, but as the home of more than half of the RAF's AAR assets in 1990 it may well now be higher on an opponents's list of priorities. No 101 Squadron flies VC10K tankers, and 216 operates multi-role tanker Tristars.

101 Squadron, commanded in 1990 by Wing Commander Geoff Simpson, has an illustrious history. It was the first night bomber unit in the Royal Flying Corps in July 1917. In the Second World War it flew Blenheims, Wellingtons and Lancasters contributing to the 1000 bomber raids of 1942 and specialising in Radio Counter Measure Operations as electronic warfare began to move centre stage in the later years of the war. It became the first Canberra squadron in 1951, subsequently re-equipping with Vulcan B1s and B2s. It has operated the VC10K tanker, converted from civilian airliners, since 1984.

At Brize Norton, the wide range of responsi-bilities of the tanker force were explained by Squadron Leader Colin Haigh, now OC Flying Support Squadron, who brings to his task the accumulated experience of 3,500 tanking hours on Victors and VC10s.

As widely publicised in the press, 101 Squadron has nine VC10K tankers, each one able to transfer up to 80 tonnes (176,000 lbs) of fuel, 50 per cent more than each Victor. Both aircraft employ the same system of three hoses: one from each wingtip and one from below the tail plane. Two aircraft refuelling simulta-neously would use the wingtip points, a single-ton usually the centre line which has a consid-erably faster rate of flow than those in the wingtips. Prodding, like every other activity in the closely integrated effort, does not happen by chance. It is the end product of meticulous planning and considerable experience.

Squadron Leader Haigh referred to the tanker squadrons as 'enablers and extenders', a unique contribution which allowed other air-craft to achieve much more on every refuelled sortie. But such was its value that the tankers were in constant demand. Headquarters Strike Command Staff allocated overall priorities between daily routine tasks throughout the RAF, exercises – which could include AAR for allied participants – joint maritime exercises and roulement of aircraft to the Falklands, North America and Cyprus. In addition, there was the daily QRA as previously described by Flight Lieutenant McLaughlin at Marham. The priorities and tasks are reviewed monthly

by the Command staff and a certain number of hours allocated to each of the three tanker squadrons. Thereafter the weekly programmes are drawn up by Operations Wing staff at Brize Norton in liaison with the units requiring tanking sorties, which would include Harriers, Jaguars and Tornado GR1s as well as the 11 Group interceptors. Over 50 per cent of tanker effort at Brize Norton is allocated to air defence related operations. Daily training sorties are doubled and trebled in duration and value as a result of AAR.

Squadron Leader Haigh explained that the fundamental principle of peacetime operation is to plan tanker sorties in such a way that the minimum fuel is consumed by the tanker itself and the maximum off loaded to the customers. A tanker will regularly refuel six or more aircraft in a 'racetrack' towline. Whereas in a QRA sortie the tanker would move to the fighter, on routine sorties the tanker stays in a predetermined location and barring emergen-cies, the number and timing of refuelling 'slots' are pre-booked by the squadrons involved. Further, to reduce fuel costs and aircraft fatigue hours, normal VC10K crew mutual continuation training is incorporated at the end of a refuelling sortie: for example, circuits and practice diversions.

In wartime the Brize Norton Squadrons would avoid any repetition of the Ju 88 experience by deploying either singly or as a squadron to bases closer to likely operating areas, both to increase survivability and further conserve integral fuel. The Sector Controller has to consider fuel consumption when he scrambles the tanker for QRA support, for the most advantageous and economic rendezvous with the fighter. A missed contact could not only jeopardise the fighter but could mean the tanker having to burn off fuel to reach safe landing weight limits. A bonus for the tanker crew however is the occasional opportunity to accompany single fighters to look at one of the intruders when they are arriving in pairs. 101 Squadron has an impressive collection of air photographs of Russian aircraft illustrating its own 'dual role' of providing additional high resolution data to the Service's intelligence bank.

Across the airfield stand the Tristars of 216 Squadron, commanded by Wing Commander

En route to armament practice camp in Cyprus. A Tristar of No 216 Squadron refuels a Phantom F4J of No 74 Squadron *(No 216 Squadron/Crown Copyright)*

Peter Hoskins. 216 was re-numbered from No 16 RNAS Squadron on 1 April 1918 and served for the remainder of the war as a long range bomber unit. From 1919 until 1955, the squadron served in the Middle and Far East, designated first as a bomber/transport squadron and then largely committed to resupply and reinforcement of ground forces. From 1956 to 1975 it flew the De Havilland Comet Mk 2 and 4, as the first military jet transport squadron. Many thousands of miles were flown in this period on Royal and VIP duties.

After a brief period flying the Buccaneer S2B bomber, the squadron assumed its present transport/tanker role at Brize Norton in 1983. In peacetime, 216 is primarily a transport squadron, but with a theoretical maximum fuel load of 141 tonnes – virtually twice the capacity of the Victor, it is a highly flexible asset for allocation by Headquarters Strike Command. Wing Commander Hoskins described the ideal role of the Tristar as a back up to the VC10K and Victor K aircraft, when the single point fuselage hose could be used to sustain other tankers rather than dispense fuel direct to the fighters. Nevertheless, when transport duties permit, the Tristar shares the QRA

support task and regularly refuels combat aircraft directly in training and exercises. Like the other tankers, the Tristar is itself equipped to be refuelled in-flight.

216 has seven Tristars of which five are equipped for AAR with a sixth due to join the squadron in the near future. In the refuelling operation there would be three men on the flight deck, with the Flight Engineer discharging the responsibility of the AEO in the Victor and VC10 of monitoring the fuel flow. A further refinement is the presence of closed circuit television to keep an eye on the prodding aircraft. Otherwise the principles and methods of operation are similar to those employed by the other tanker squadrons, all working to standards and guidelines agreed among NATO allies.

In war, the role allocation to 216 would be decided at a very high level, depending on the relative priorities to be awarded to AAR or transport. Whatever the proportions contributed by 216, the overall impact of AAR on fighter squadron operations would be enormous. Combat air patrols and interceptions would be limited only by weapon consumption and crew endurance. All four fighter wings

QRA Shackleton of No 8 Squadron at Lossiemouth *(Author)*

could be concentrated at any critical point in the battle anywhere in the UKADR from either their main or dispersed airfields. What would Air Marshal Dowding have given for such a facility in 1940?

Airborne Early Warning

In the following chapter the extensive contributions to UK air defence by the inheritance of the Chain Home responsibilities are described. But a very important innovation since 1940 is the provision of airborne early warning by aircraft equipped with many of the installations previously available only on the ground. In 1990 that responsibility for the RAF is provided by No 8 Squadron whose venerable Shackleton Mk II are about to be replaced by Boeing E3D Airborne Warning and Control aircraft, which are now already beginning work-up from the Boeing Seattle production lines.

In 1971 it was decided to enhance radar early warning for both the United Kingdom and for elements of the Fleet operating in home waters by modifying a number of Shackleton Mark II, maritime reconnaissance air-craft. With an endurance of up to 12 hours, over a combat radius of 2,500 miles, the Shackleton was ideally suited for its new task. The APS 20 radar was transferred from its previous operator, the Fleet Air Arm Fairey Gannet and No 8 AEW Squadron was formed at Lossiemouth. No 8 had a distinguished fighter ground attack history, culminating with Hunter FGA 9s flying in the Middle East.

The operational value of the airborne early warning lies in its greatly extended provision of long range detection of incoming targets. Longer warning time means that fighters can be placed on CAPs which are likely to be directly in the path of incoming raids. In 1940, by comparison, it was by no means certain that all enemy attacks would be detected quickly enough by the Chain Home stations. As a result, standing patrols were frequently mounted, especially in the earlier days of convoy protection, which never made contact with the enemy. The switch of attacks by the Luftwaffe on 7 September to London has already been described. The relevance here is that such concentration and subsequent re-peated concentration, on one target, not only reduced pressure on the fighter airfields, but made the early warning task of the Chain Home stations much simpler. On the other hand, only those ground stations in south-east England could contribute whose radars could look over the Channel to the skies over north-eastern France; those further along the coast were out of range. In 1990 the AEW aircraft would be themselves directed to the combat areas wherever they occurred in the UKADR. As a result, a smaller number of fighters can be vectored with greater responsiveness and timing. Flying at 10,000 feet, the Shackleton radar horizon is extended up to 140 miles, which allows low level detection up to 200 miles. In peacetime the majority of 8 Squadron's sorties are flown over the north-eastern Atlantic and the northern North Sea working with Northern Sector at Buchan, identifying, reporting on and tracking movements in the UKADR.

Flight Lieutenant Kim Coxon is a typical Shackleton skipper who has amassed 3,500 hours on Nimrods and Shackletons. His description of flying an aircraft whose antecedents lie in the Lancasters of the Second World War would be very evocative to old hands from RAF Bomber Command. The Shackleton cruises at about 200 mph in sorties usually extending from 7 to 10 hours. The autopilot is rudimentary and requires constant monitoring. Without modern power assisted controls, the aircraft is heavy to handle and requires constant hands-on flying. Its speed and power restrict opportunities to fly either round or above bad weather and, as the author himself experienced on previous occasions, noise levels are high and temperature highly variable. For most effective radar projection, Flight Lieutenant Coxon must constantly be aware of thermal and haze layers and achieve the best position for maximum signal and communication range. He must be as responsive to changing operational circumstances as his fighter and tanker colleagues, minimising by precise flying the differences in aircraft performance. Meanwhile his navigator, Flight Lieutenant Dave McAra, would be lacking the modern navigational computers of the F3 and would confirm the aircraft's position in a specified 10 mile corridor by taking periodic astro shots from a hand held sextant. Although frequently at low level, the Shackleton navigator has no visual ground cross references when

operating 1,000 miles out over the Atlantic.

Although the pilot is always in command of the aircraft, the actual operations will be controlled by the Tactical Director, or TACO. The senior TACO, and Squadron Leader 'operations' on 8 Squadron is Squadron Leader Mike Frankland who has been working with AEW aircraft in Britain and the United States since he first joined 8 Squadron in 1974. He gave an insight into the contribution of the Shackleton as the third member of the fighter-tanker-AEW QRA team.

The squadron is held at readiness states similar to those of the tankers and in peacetime will also receive from Buchan an early indication of possible 'trade'. The TACO would be given the expected time of penetration of the UKADR by the 'X-ray', the position of the appropriate 'barrier' position to be taken up by the Shackleton and details of other assets involved including both aircraft and ships. The Shackleton's 'scramble' may lack the reheated surge of the Tornado but it remains a formidable spectacle as the aircraft climbs away over the Moray Firth with an urgency that belies its years. Transit to the 'barrier' could take up to three hours: a fact which reflects the early warning now available to the United Kingdom from allied units well beyond the UKADR. In the first 30 minutes the TACO and his four controller/operators will be extremely busy ensuring that generator, radar and all communications are working efficiently. As the Shackleton may itself be below ground radar coverage it is essential that both visual and radar lookout is maintained, especially in the vicinity of the North Sea oilfields, with their heavy helicopter and light aircraft traffic.

The TACO tells the Sector Operations Centre when the Shackleton has reached its barrier position and begins its lookout. In peacetime, the X-rays would almost certainly be tracked by one agency after the other, with the Shackleton crew aware of their progress. Sometimes, however, contact could be lost and the TACO has to decide whether it is necessary to change position to fly across the intruders' expected track. Occasionally, communications with the other friendly agencies may also be lost, as could very well happen in war, and again the TACO's experience and judgement would be required. Squadron

Leader Frankland recalled one occasion when he was told to expect a Bear in five minutes on a bearing of 020° at a distance of 200 miles. Ten minutes later a Bear was identified 60° off, 100 miles closer and heading in a different direction. As he quickly decided to inform the fighter-tanker combination, a second image appeared on the screen in exactly the forecast position. In the battle of wits, the intruders are likely to know roughly where the Shackleton is, and they are training to confuse it and measure its responses.

Once the X-rays have been identified and all details passed back to the SOC, the Shackleton crew may head for home, or shadow the Bears if they are *en route* into the Atlantic bound for Cuba or West Africa, or remain on station if more X-rays are expected.

The Shackleton will be cruising in its barrier position at half the speed of the intercepting fighter, but the speed of events is common to all the participants. The TACO and his colleagues cannot sit back and wait for things to happen. The most meticulous planning can be negated by the unexpected, be it equipment failure, communications breakdown or a particularly skilfull and wily intruder. Tactical awareness, swift and accurate decisions and operational flexibility are demanded from all the nine man team on board the aircraft.

But whatever the affection felt for the Shackleton by her crews, all are looking forward to its imminent replacement by the E3D Sentry. In 1990 a group of specialists at RAF Waddington were preparing the operational training programme for the imminent arrival of the first RAF AWACS. Sentry comprises a Boeing 707 airframe, with aircraft instrumentation dating from that generation, powered by four General Electric/Snecma Consortium CF 56 turbofan engines giving 24,000 lbs of thrust each and mounting a Westinghouse radome and ancillary radar, control and communications equipment based on advanced computer systems. It carries a flight deck crew of four and a mission team 'down the back' of 13.

The most obvious internal difference between the Shackleton and the Sentry is available space. In the Shackleton one climbs over the main spar to move between cockpit and systems operator, squeezes past the Tactical

Coordinator and his colleagues and does not need to move very far to finish up in the constricted space near the tailplane. In Sentry, all the main consoles and 13 operators are in what in the original 707 would have been the first class compartment. The centre and rear fuselage accommodate the Radar Technician, computer, storage cabinets, signal processors and a great deal of other equipment associated with the radome above the fuselage, still leaving plenty of room for movement about the aircraft, spare seating, bunks and the indispensable galley. As a result, despite some individual items weighing several hundred pounds, the designers have had the space to include many duplicate systems which have greatly enhanced operational reliability.

The contrast between the internal characteristics of Shackleton and Sentry symbolises their differences in operating capacity and operational impact on UK Air Defence. Flight Lieutenant Stan Davies, an Air Electronics Officer and Tactical Director in the Sentry Training Squadron at RAF Waddington described how the aircraft's radar could 'see' for well in excess of 250 miles from its usual operating height of about 30,000 feet. An unrefuelled patrol could last for 13 hours, with time on station depending on its distance from base at a maximum speed of more than 500 mph. Such capacity means that Sentry's operational radius could extend beyond a sector boundary or even beyond the UKADR itself. The entry into RAF service of seven E3Ds before the end of March 1992 probably marks the biggest single improvement in United Kingdom air defence since the original Chain Home stations were built at the outbreak of the Second World War. The E3D is equipped with realtime secure communication data links between radar stations, air defence commanders, the fleet, interceptors, tankers and allied aircraft and ground agencies. Automatic Data handling and signal processing capacity is such that a very large volume of traffic can be monitored and controlled over many hundreds of square miles of sky. In sum, the advent of the E3D will facilitate the integration of all NATO's airborne early warning assets: USAF, NATO and French Air Force, with associated ground agencies, to an unprecedented extent.

E3D Sentry on trials *(Boeing)*

As always, effective operation depends on the skills and teamwork of a large number of aircrew and groundcrew. Usually Sentry will fly with 17 people on board: four on the flight deck and the remainder, known collectively as the 'mission crew' down the back. For the first time in the modern RAF, aircrew will also be drawn from ground branch officers and ground tradesmen. Under the overall direction of the Tactical Director are three teams: one responsible for allocation and control of weapons (i.e. interceptors and, perhaps, in the future, surface to air missiles) one for surveillance, and one for communications, all backed up by three technician specialists: displays, radar and communications.

At Waddington the Training Squadron's Fighter Allocator and deputy Mission Crew leader is Squadron Leader Mike Sellar from the Fighter Control Ground Branch. His job in the air is to be fully aware of the details of the hostile threat and of the friendly forces available to him for their intercept in order to supervise target allocation, manning of fighter CAPS and the scramble of fighters. He in turn leads and supervises two Weapons Controllers whose tasks resemble those of the Intercept Controller at the ground station with the additional need to capitalise fully the detection capability of Sentry. Their product is the accurate placing of the fighter to intercept an identified track. In the Battle of Britain that would have been equal to intercepting German bombers as they took off from their airfields in northern France and Denmark at the same time. All three members of the Fighter Allocator/Weapons Controller team are likely to be Fighter Controllers and could include females.

Seated in the adjacent bank of consoles, next to the Tactical Director, is the Surveillance

Controller, who leads a team of Surveillance Operators. He could be a member of the Fighter Control Branch or a navigator or AEO. Flight Lieutenant Gil Stenson at Waddington joined the Fighter Control Branch in 1984 after service as a navigator, latterly on 8 Squadron, so he brings a valuable experience blend to his training design duties. He explains his objective as 'giving the ground the earliest possible warning of attack by ensuring that radar can see as far as possible'. That usually means scanning the electronic spectrum across an area of sky 1,000 miles in diameter – virtually the distance between Lands End and John O'Groats using several sensors in one aircraft. The systems can track targets automatically but Flight Lieutenant Stenson believes that a well trained operator could very probably pick up a manoeuvring track before the computer had time to register it. Of particular significance could be a high speed track heading straight for Sentry itself. Such a critically important air defence asset would inevitably become a high value target to an opposition. Usually, friendly fighters would be positioned between the E3D and the threat, but the surveillance operators must have a finely developed sense of tactical awareness as well as interpretive skills on the screen. The Data Link system is also under the supervision of the Surveillance Controller, as are ESM and IFF equipment.

In peacetime, as in war, the Weapons and Surveillance teams will work closely together to monitor and control practice interception. The Surveillance Controller can choose from a number of range scales which he can instantly change while continuing to monitor all. Similarly, while a practice interception is being run, his Operators can look elsewhere to continue to supervise and advise on all tracks within the Sentry's area of interest in order to keep the 'Recognised Air and Surface Picture' up to date.

The third team comprises the Communications Operator and the Communications Technician. Without communications, Sentry is deaf, dumb and useless. The Communications Operator works directly for the Tactical Director (TD) and aircraft commander. Before the mission he will confirm the cooperating agencies and determine which links and communications will be required. All crew members will make bids for communicating channels and with the TD he will determine priorities and set up a communications plan. In transit to station he will load all communications software, tune up the stations, make contact with the cooperating agencies and then hand over the various channels to his crew colleagues. Thereafter he will monitor as many sets as possible and listen for jamming. Where there is no automatic response he will be responsible for appropriate counter measures.

Master Air Electronics Operator Bob Harrison, Communications Operator at Waddington, compared his early days in the service as a Hastings signaller when he was responsible for one HF, one UHF and one VHF set, all manually tuned, with his current responsibilities for three HF, two VHF and 14 UHF sets communicating constantly with several ground units, a naval task force, fighters, tankers and other AEW aircraft. He happily observed that the E3D galley was also far better equipped than that of the Hastings.

The size of the Sentry easily accommodates three technicians whose job is to monitor and, wherever possible, effect in-flight repairs or replacement to all the mission related equipment. The Communications Technician obviously works closely with the Communications Operator. The Display Technician, as his title indicates, is responsible for the efficient production by the computer of the displays required by the Weapons and Surveillance operators. This involves monitoring and in-flight maintenance of data processing, data display, and the on-board self test system. He will usually be a Sergeant with a new RAF trade specialisation: Flight Systems and Air Radar Technician.

Because of the interdependence of all crew members, the aircraft's effectiveness would be impaired by the loss of any single one. If, however, the main radar, in its 30 feet diameter rotodome, mounted 11 feet above the fuselage, should malfunction, the aircraft would completely fail in its operational purpose.

Since joining the Service as an apprentice, Chief Technician Bill Barrie has worked for 20 years on the ground as an electronic air radar technician. Now he is about to wear a flying brevet and talks as enthusiastically about the demands of aircrew cooperation, emergency procedures and airmanship as he does about his task of ensuring that the Sentry stays awake throughout the sortie. If automatic redundancy procedures do not correct a fault, he can run a diagnostic tape which will indicate what has failed and he can replace specific units from limited spares held on board. During return to base, he can run a further maintenance check which automatically confirms any previous faults and prepares a comprehensive debrief for the guidance of the groundcrew in further repairs or replacements. He has no-one to delegate his responsibilities to and must maintain constant vigilance throughout the sortie. Not surprisingly he is enthusiastic about the new horizon which has literally opened to men of his hitherto earth bound trade.

Such is the complexity of the operations going on down 'the back end' that it is easy to forget that all this is taking place at 30,000 feet at speeds in excess of 400 knots. Keeping a watchful eye from the cockpit on all the traditional flight systems of a large multi-engined aircraft is Flight Sergeant John Warrilow, a flight engineer with several thousand hours on the Nimrod maritime reconnaissance aircraft, on the ill-fated Nimrod AEW and now on Sentry. His pre-flight checks are similar to those carried out daily by flight engineers across the RAF, starting 1½ hours before take off. Beginning with external examination of the airframe, he moves systematically through the outer and inner shells of the aircraft looking for tell tale signs of leaks or disconnected electrics. Although the Sentry has modern equipment down the back, it is essentially an airframe with instrumentation of an earlier era, but complicated aerodynamically by the radome and the powerful engines. He must cover all 'air vehicle' systems: hydraulics, pneumatics, oxygen, pressurisation, electrics, throttle handling and instrument cross checks as well as the engines.

All must be monitored throughout the flight, especially the fuel state and the impact of any changes to the pre-planned flight profile. He has no direct responsibility for the mission equipment but works closely with the three technicians to ensure that the rotordome is set to the required rotation speed and that all electrical and air conditioning systems are

functioning smoothly. He must also be ready to carry out any routine maintenance should the aircraft land away from base. In sum, he too is unlikely to find time weighing heavily on his hands in an 11 hour sortie.

Finally, up in the left hand seat is the first pilot who would also be the aircraft captain. In any future conflict Sentry would be in the front line. It would not be dogfighting like a Hurricane or Spitfire; it would not be silently lying in ambush for the incoming bombers and their escorts like the Tornado or Phantom. If things should go horrendously wrong, and a determined enemy fighter armed with anti-radiation missiles should break through to attack the E3D, the captain would have only his flying skills and tactical awareness to ensure the survival of his exceptionally valuable aircraft and 17 crew members. Wherever possible, those 17 men, and women, will fly as a 'constituted' crew. It was particularly pleasing to hear Flight Lieutenant Dick Geddes, a senior pilot on the E3D training team, emphasise the irreplaceable value of teamwork, and by implication of leadership, in the air within one aircraft. Leadership is manifest in many forms in combat: at its most dramatic in the skills and character of men like Bader, Malan, Hull and Thompson. The amalgam of qualities to produce leadership in war is complex and occasionally controversial, but professional skill, bravery, example and awareness of the needs of subordinates and colleagues are usually at the top of the list. As the E3D enters into service, the task of welding 17 individuals of different ranks and backgrounds into a finely honed team capable of maintaining operational effectiveness under fire, or the threat of it, will present a new challenge to Flight Lieutenant Geddes' colleagues.

*   *   *

And so, in any future conflict, the front line squadrons of 11 Group would bear the brunt of the battle as their predecessors did in 1940. They are even fewer than the men singled out by Winston Churchill. There can be no substitute for individual skill and aircraft capability. In 1990 the skills have been considerably more refined as a result of the work of the Wyton Canberras and the capability of each fighter has been extended by the contribution of the tankers and the AEW aircraft.

Chapter Six

GROUNDWORK

As THE HURRICANE and Spitfire pilots wakened before dawn in the critical late August and early September days of 1940 their thoughts would no doubt be on the sorties, and odds, waiting for them in the skies over south-east England. A few yards away, across the grass, stood the awaiting Spitfires and Hurricanes already fuelled, armed and with the previous day's damage, wherever possible, patched and repaired. Around the coast the night watches of the Chain Home radar stations followed the last of the solitary plots of German raiders returning, usually unopposed, to their bases in northern France and the low countries. The crews of Sir Tim Pile's searchlight and gun batteries relaxed as they prepared to hand over the major responsibility to the fighter pilots.

In the peaceful skies of 1990, the vast majority of the men and women of 11 Group would still be sleeping peacefully at 3 a.m. Only a handful of Phantoms and Tornadoes would be stationed silently in floodlit HAS, with the QRA aircrew resting within earshot of the communications line from their Sector Operations Centre. Nearby the four or five groundcrew responsible for the preparation of the aircraft would also be sleeping, secure in the knowledge that their aircraft were ready to launch, like their Spitfire and Hurricane predecessors, fuelled and armed to challenge any intruder.

Just as in 1940, the air battle would be decided by the aircrew. 'Kill or be killed', 'Be there and cope', would not simply be stern cliches from TWU combat instructors, but once again the reality of war in the air. But without the guidance of the ground control centres the aircrew would be unlikely to 'be there' when it mattered. Even with competent ground control it is possible that some raider would penetrate the fighter screen. If they did, they would be engaged by the surface-to-air missiles and guns of the RAF's Bloodhound, Rapier and Skyguard batteries. All would be supported by groundcrew whose training, competence and enthusiasm is worthy of their combat ready colleagues.

Ground Control

In 1990 the air defence assets of 11 Group are controlled via a network of control centres, radars, computers and communications data links collectively known as The United Kingdom Air Defence Ground Environment, referred to colloquially as UKADGE. Control devolves from AOC 11 Group as the air defence commander, through two main Sector Operations Centres, one Northern and one Southern to a number of Control and Reporting Centres whose title indicates their responsibilities. These are the descendants of the Chain Home Radio Detection Finding Stations (RDF) associated with the inventive genius of Sir Robert Watson-Watt and a colleague Mr A F Wilkins in the mid-1930s which made air-to-air defence against bombers a feasible proposition. In 1935, a Handley Page Heyford bomber was flown in the path of a radio beam transmitted from the BBC's station at Daventry and a receiver linked to a cathode ray oscilloscope showed it displacing the returning signal by a quantifiable amount. Thereby the potential of detection by radio signals was proved. At that time, Air Marshal Dowding was the Air Member of the RAF Council responsible for research and development and took a strong personal interest in applying the invention to air defence. Special transmitters were built at Orfordness and later at Bawdsey in Suffolk, where the twin 250 foot lattice masts became a familiar landmark. By 1937 three stations had been built and skilled operators were accurately identifying the distance and bearing of incoming 'raids', although accurate heights were not so easy to ascertain. By February 1940, 29 stations were operational, ranging the British coastline from Cornwall round the east of England and Scotland up to Scapa Flow.

As the Chain Home stations rapidly increased, the need for operators quickly outstripped supply and in November 1939 Women's Auxiliary Air Force volunteers were recruited and quickly demonstrated a very high level of competence. As the Luftwaffe came to realise the importance of the CH stations they

were heavily attacked but, despite serious casualties on several occasions, the WAAF operators were never found wanting, meriting a signal from the AOC-in-C in August expressing 'his satisfaction on how the WAAF personnel had withstood the air attacks.'

Principles of surveillance, reporting and control have changed little over 50 years. Modern radar capacity and communication nets however mean that far heavier traffic over a far greater range can be handled by a handful of stations. In 1940 details on an incoming raid: position, numbers, altitude and direction

Below: The United Kingdom Air Defence Region showing the sector operations centres, control and reporting posts
Right: Marconi Type 91 Mobile Phased Array Radar D Band Surveillance with lateral IFF aerial on top *(Marconi)*

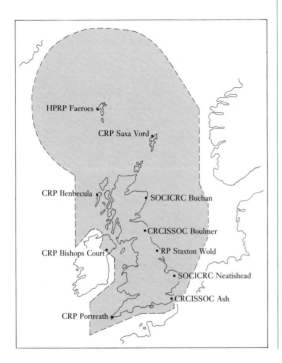

would be passed by direct telephone line to a 'Filter' room at Group Headquarters. There, knowledge of the location of friendly forces would lead to classification of friendly, hostile or unidentified, the 'X-raid' antecedent of the modern 'X-ray'. Details of hostiles and X-rays would be passed simultaneously to Operations Rooms at Fighter Command, Group and Sector where they were plotted by WAAF on the large map tables familiar from countless photographs and films. Often the same raids would be reported by more than one adjacent CH station from their radar ranges of 100 miles and the Group Filter staff, by using more than one 'fix', could pinpoint enemy aircraft with considerable accuracy.

Then the raids would be allocated by Group to the Sector Operations Centres (SOC) who, in turn, would exercise control over a number of squadrons. For example, on 1 July 1940, Biggin Hill Sector controlled 32 and 79 Hurricane squadrons at Biggin Hill, 245 Squadron's Hurricanes at Hawkinge, 600 Squadron's Blenheims at Manston and 610 Squadron's Spitfires at Gravesend. On 1 September, North Weald Sector controlled 25

Squadron's Blenheims at Martlesham Heath, 56 Squadron's Hurricanes at North Weald and 151 Squadron's remaining Hurricanes at Stapleford before they were withdrawn to Digby later in the day in exchange for 46 Squadron.

The order to scramble would come by telephone from the SOC direct to the squadron crewroom: the precursor of the open line from SOC to QRA HAS in 1990. Then it was usually the whole squadron which was scrambled, or at least a flight of six Spitfires or Hurricanes, as the incoming raids after 12 August usually comprised 50 or more fighters and bombers and frequently more than 300. Sometimes the CH stations had identified so many incoming raids that the SOCs simply gave a general heading and a broad directive to their fighters: 'Patrol behind Dover and engage enemy fighters . . .'

While the importance of the CH stations was quickly realised by the Luftwaffe and heavy attacks launched against them, it seems that the critical contribution of the sector airfields, co-locating both SOC and squadrons, was never fully appreciated. Had Biggin Hill, North Weald, Kenley, Hornchurch and the others been singled out for concentrated repeated attacks the impact on the overall defensive would have been extremely grave. Dislocation of the CH net, although occasionally serious was relieved by the installation of mobile units, but elimination of the SOCs would have blinded all their dependent squadrons or overloaded alternative controllers. As it was, the controllers' task was complex enough. Too early a scramble could mean precious fuel being consumed in loiter time with consequent detriment to combat endurance. Too late and the bombers could be through to their targets and the climbing fighters themselves bounced by the escorting ME 109s. Like the principles, the fundamental problems remain in 1990. But just as aircrew training has benefited from the lessons of 1940, so has the preparation of UKADGE.

RAF Buchan is the location of the Northern Sector Operations Centre. The SOC lies deep underground near the Aberdeenshire coast, well away from any airfield. It controls the Leuchars and Leeming Tornado Wings, the Shackletons of No 8 Squadron and the Scottish Rapier SAMs at Leuchars and Losiemouth. It directs the operations of Boulmer, Saxa Vord and Benbecula Control and Reporting centres and the Danish radar station in the Faeroes.

Sector Commander at Buchan is Group Captain Nick Buckley, who flew Lightnings with 74 Squadron before transferring to the General Duties (Fighter Control) Branch after losing his aircrew medical category in 1972. Since then he has served as intercept controller, display controller and master controller at Saxa Vord, Benbecula and Boulmer. His responsibilities in wartime would closely resemble those of his predecessors at Biggin Hill and North Weald, except that his area of responsibility and available assets are many times greater. Northern Sector is two or three times the size of Southern. Whereas the latter is closely involved with allied air forces across the Channel and southern North Sea, the Buchan Sector stretches out beyond the Faeroes and across to the Scandinavian air defence boundary.

As a result, Buchan operations have a strongly maritime flavour and are usually at long range. In addition to the RAF units already mentioned, several Royal Navy ships have air defence responsibilities. When these are operating within Buchan's area of responsibility, C-in-C Fleet and AOC-in-C Strike Command, as C-in-C UK Air would agree on the category of Coordinated Air Sea Procedures to be allocated to them. If tactical control of a ship's air defence activities was allocated to Buchan, the Sector Controller could either allocate CAP aircraft to it for control, or simply sustain communications links and use the mobility of the ship to plug any gaps in the Sector air defence picture. This close air defence relationship between the Royal Navy and the RAF when the fleet is in home waters is further strengthened by the wartime allocation of Nos 11 and 29 Squadrons to Supreme Allied Commander Atlantic. Both squadrons would, if necessary, deploy from their bases at Leeming and Coningsby to airfields closer to their maritime area of operations.

The greatly extended range of modern radars, complemented by the combat radius and in-flight refuelling of the F3s and F4s and now to be increased even more by the advent of E3D Sentry, allows a very flexible concept of

The northernmost link in the 1990 home chain. The radar domes of RAF Saxa Vord *(Author)*

operations to be implemented by Group Captain Buckley. In times when hostilities are imminent, Buchan would have as first priority the provision of an accurate picture of the air environment to the Air Defence Commander in the War Headquarters at High Wycombe, i.e. the responsibility borne in 1940 by the CH stations. Reaction to hostile acts and rules of engagement would be determined above Sector level. Pursuing the 1940 parallel, scrambling orders to the Leuchars and Leeming wings could be given by the co-located Control and Reporting Centre (CRC) at Buchan. The CRC has a master controller responsible for constructing his local air picture and would assume tactical control of fighters allocated to it. Once scrambled, the fighters could be handed over to smaller radar installations, the Control and Reporting Posts, for final control of CAPs and intercepts.

As explained in previous chapters, the scrambling of QRA sorties closely resembles, up to the point of intercept, the actual control in war of the fighter squadrons. In the case of Flight Lieutenant McDonald Webb's 'Bear hunt' of November 1989 for example, the interception was handled by RAF Saxa Vord, the northernmost RAF station at the top end of the Shetland Isles: the Cold War equivalent of Rye CH and Biggin Hill SOC, watching for intruders from around the North Cape. The

routine 'ops' briefing that morning for the unit commander, Squadron Leader Brian Gregson, was interrupted with the news from Norwegian allies that two X-rays had rounded the Cape and appeared to be heading towards the UKADR.

In the darkened operations room there was an air of expectancy and the screens were scanned in complete silence with even greater keenness than usual. Shortly after 8 o'clock Senior Aircraftsman Karl Moran, the duty tracker plotter, first spotted the two faint blips which were indeed heading for the Air Defence Region boundary. Meanwhile the progress of Flight Lieutenant McDonald Webb and Flight Lieutenant Heaton northwards from Leeming was being monitored back at Buchan and the Victor tanker from 55 Squadron was on its way from Marham. SAC Moran confirmed the location of the incoming aircraft and informed the CRC at Buchan and Flying Officer Laird McKay, looking cooler than perhaps he felt, took over the F3 from Buchan and prepared to control his first QRA intercept. The F3 was turned north–eastwards towards the incoming blips; the timing was such that there was no need to hold it on CAP. After a couple of minutes Flight Lieutenant McDonald Webb reported that he had radar contact and confirmed that the F3 crew and Pilot Officer McKay were looking at the same

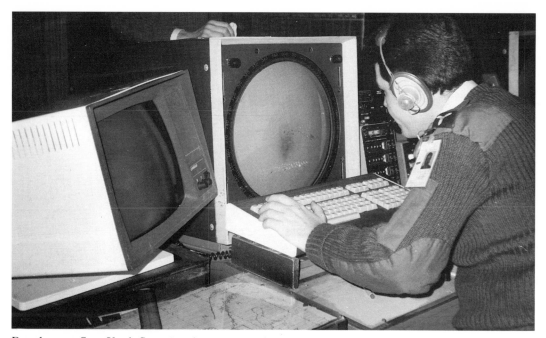

Bear hunt at Saxa Vord: Scanning the screen in the operations room *(Author)*

two targets. Visual identification soon followed: two Soviet Naval Air Force Bear D
reconnaissance aircraft. That was what all the
Saxa Vord ops room team had expected, but
the smoothly coordinated identification gave
greater satisfaction, especially to Flying Officer
McKay.

The control staff watched on the screens as
the Tornado widened the angle between itself
and the Bears. Then, as the Russians crossed
ahead, it swung rapidly round to starboard
behind the second aircraft. The blips steadily
closed as Flight Lieutenant McDonald Webb
moved up to photographic range. For several
minutes all three blips moved southwards
together across the radar screen while another,
the Victor tanker, made its appearance from
the south. Then the Bears began a lazy wide
angle turn which was to take them out of the
UKADR and back towards the North Cape.
Flight Lieutenant McDonald Webb confirmed
his disengagement with Flying Officer McKay
and began a routine link up with the tanker
before returning to base. As the blips separated, two more appeared on the north-east
edge of the screen, swiftly moving and
obviously heading towards the Bears. These
were identified as two Royal Norwegian Air
Force F16s, to provide a further escort for the

Bears' return loop round the North Cape.

The picture on the screen was far superior to
that available in 1940. The range of the Type
96 surveillance radar at Saxa Vord was far
greater and communications were much
clearer. Moreover, had there been any problems at Saxa Vord the Master Controller at
Buchan CRC had been monitoring the entire
operation and was available for back up. How
would such effectiveness be achieved in combat, when the intruders would not be so
nonchalantly predictable, when their numbers
and direction could be concealed by ECM,
when not three but thirty blips could be appearing on the Saxa Vord and Buchan screens?
The answer lies in the modern application of
techniques pioneered in 1939 and 1940.

For example, Pilot Officer Michelle Taylor
is an Identification and Recognition Officer
(IDRO) at Buchan CRC. She must be able to
identify all aircraft tracks in her area of
responsibility. She will have information passed from friendly agencies: Southern Sector
Operations Centre at Neatishead, NATO
allies, and Prestwick for information on any
civilian flights. She must be able to separate
friend from foe, relying on technical means and
procedures which require her to be aware of
track behaviour. Obviously, a high degree of

skill and judgement has to be brought to bear. She would be assisted by a Sergeant supervisor, two operators who produce detailed information on tracks not yet identified by the forward CRPs and two others who monitor all movements. Pilot Officer Taylor summarised the issues at stake: 'An IDRO mistake is embarrassing in peacetime but would be fatal in war.'

Pilot Officer Taylor's information would be passed to the Track Production Officer (TPO) who would have been located in 1940 at the Group Filter Room, but is now also at the Control Reporting Centre. The TPO is responsible for producing an air picture for Air Defence Commanders at all levels, and at Buchan covers an area up to 250 miles north of the Faeroes. In 1940 that information would have travelled to a third location: the Sector Operations Centre, say at Biggin Hill, for the fighters to be allocated. At Buchan it is simply passed across to the Fighter Allocator who, under the broad direction of the Master Controller, actually allocates targets within raids to specific squadrons. Thus a comprehensive but closely coordinated sequence is completed: individual track identification; creation of overall air defence picture; allocation of fighters. The chain is completed when the scrambled fighter is taken over by the Intercept Controller, but the responsibilities of the Fighter Allocator have only just begun. In wartime, CAPS would almost certainly be mounted rather then individual scrambles against each incoming raid. The Fighter Allocator must therefore ensure that he keeps the master controller up to date with CAP aircraft fuel and weapons states to ensure that they are either replenished or replaced in good time.

Flying Officer Simon Smith is, like Flying Officer McKay at Saxa Vord, an Intercept Controller. In the 'Bear hunt' described above, Flying Officer McKay brought the F3 to a position from which the X-ray could be identified. Flying Officer Smith explained how, in both regular and peacetime exercises and in war, the intercept controller would place the fighter in a position to bring his weapons to bear. When working with a Phantom or Tornado, he could exercise relatively loose control, giving the fighter crew sufficient range data for them to work out their own intercepts.

The Hawk however has no on-board AI radar and must therefore be more closely controlled if it is not in close proximity to the all-weather fighters. The Hawk pilot may be flying a low level CAP prepared for a visual interception using AIM 9L heat-seeking missiles and guns, or he may be flying a defensive pattern behind the Tornadoes and Phantoms to pick off any intruders who have penetrated the forward screen. In either case, he will require very accurate indication of the location, direction and height of the 'Bogeys'. When there are also friendly fighters out ahead of him he must be given all possible assistance by the intercept controller for accurate and timely IFF. Indeed, Hawk air defence operations would very closely resemble those of 1940, depending on timely and accurate ground control, visual identification and close quarter attack. The Hawk is difficult to spot, especially at low level, because of its small size, which together with its very high manoeuvrability and acceleration, make it a challenging customer for the controller but a distinctly awkward one for an opponent.

Some of the Hawks could be deployed in the Southern Sector of the UK Air Defence Region, in which case they would be controlled from the Sector Operations Centre at RAF Neatishead on the Norfolk coast. Whereas operations in the Northern Sector have a distinctly maritime atmosphere, the Southern Sector covers not only the central and southern approaches to Britain but also protects the back door to central Europe. The land based strategy of the Supreme Allied Commander Europe is therefore a major influence on likely air operations.

Like Buchan, Neatishead is commanded by an officer of the General Duties (Fighter Control) Branch: Group Captain George Keith. Group Captain Keith, like most of his fighter controllers, has always been a ground branch officer, a fact that reflects the high degree of specialist skill required to discharge these particular responsibilities. Indeed, a previous incumbent of Group Captain Keith's appointment was a female Fighter Controller.

The responsibilities of Neatishead extend across the centre of England round the southeast, south and south–western coasts taking in roughly the areas of Nos 10, 11 and 12 Groups

F Flight of No 85 Squadron Bloodhounds at Wyton *(Author)*

in 1940. One unusual outpost is at RAF Bishops Court in Northern Ireland, a Control and Reporting Post which looks out over the seaward approaches to the Irish landmass. The range of modern bombers is such that Bishops Court could actually be in the front line should any opponent seek to outflank the eastward and northern looking defences. In addition, Bishops Court would have a vital role to play in safeguarding North Atlantic reinforcement routes, exactly as in the Second World War.

The tasks of the Master Controller (MC) are similar in each sector. Squadron Leader Allan Connarty is one of the MCs at Neatishead. He is typical of his generation in that, whereas his predecessor of 1940 would probably have been a reluctant transfer from aircrew, Squadron Leader Connarty has developed his expertise in a variety of ground controller appointments since he joined the RAF in 1974. His predecessor at the Sector Operations Centre in 1940 would recognise similar problems and similar techniques. Now, however, the Master Controller's task is far more complex and covers a much wider area. No longer does he study the disposition of the air battle on a large plotting table. Instead he uses computer systems which exchange air picture data, via digital links with neighbouring radar sites in the United Kingdom and on the Continent. The Master Controller must have a sound understanding of radar theory and the management of his information systems to enable him to exploit to the full the vast amount of early warning information available to him.

Surface-to-Air Defences

On 15 May 1940 Mr Churchill wrote to President Roosevelt of the United States asking for urgent American assistance. He identified a need for 3,893 light and a further 2,464 medium anti-aircraft guns. Twelve months later, despite both American assistance and rapid domestic production, AA Command was still over 3,500 guns short of the Prime Minister's Target. Nonetheless, during the period of the Battle of Britain, AA Command was credited with the destruction of 296 aircraft.

In 1990 the fighter squadrons are supplemented by the Bloodhound II Surface-to-Air Missiles (SAM) of No 85 Squadron, five Rapier short range missile squadrons, and two

Flt Lt Sue Gilroy, Engagement Controller, 85 Squadron, Wattisham on Bloodhound control consol *(Author)*

Royal Auxiliary Air Force squadrons armed with Oerlikon AA guns.

In the Bloodhound squadron a very distinguished number plate is preserved. 85 Squadron fought throughout the Battle of Britain in the North Weald and Kenley Sectors under the command of Squadron Leader, later Group Captain Peter Townsend DSO, DFC and Bar. It was finally withdrawn from the front line on 3 September exhausted and, like every other squadron withdrawn in those critical days, protesting violently to the AOC. Even by the illustrious standards of its contemporaries, its claims of 141 enemy aircraft destroyed and 64 damaged were outstanding, as was its tally of decorations: two DSO's, 10 DFC's, two DFM's, a bar to the DFC and a bar to the DFM, as well as an MBE for the squadron's engineer officer. The cost had been heavy: 18 pilots killed, several injured and many others shot down but surviving to fight another day.

In 1990 there is a very different kind of squadron membership: the Engagement Controllers of the missiles and their supporting ground technicians. 85 Squadron is deployed from its Headquarters at West Raynham in six Flights. The Engagement Controllers are drawn from both General Duties (Flying) and General Duties (Fighter Control) Branches, and could be officers, warrant officers or SNCOs. The Controllers complete a 10 week training course at West Raynham before taking post on one of the Squadron's Flights.

At Wattisham, the deputy commander of E Flight is Flight Lieutenant Sue Gilroy, a member of the Fighter Control Branch with previous experience, like her colleague Pilot Officer Michelle Taylor at Buchan, as Identification and Reporting Officer in ground radar operations. As an Engagement Controller she is responsible for firing the Bloodhound missile. The Wattisham Flight is under the tactical control of the Sector Operations Centre at Neatishead, and Flight Lieutenant Gilroy, together with her colleagues would have targets allocated to the battery by Neatishead or would use the battery's own radar in a search mode to locate its own. It provides a second line of area defence overland behind the fighter screens. Several of the batteries share airfields with RAF aircraft and all the controllers are fully aware of the need for accurate IFF and close coordination not just with AD fighters but with friendly attack aircraft returning to home bases. Although in RAF service since 1964, Bloodhound has been frequently up-graded, most recently receiving a major computer refit. The battery's Target Illuminating Radar tracks a target, locks on and the Bloodhound missile is primed to home on to the specific signal reflected from it. It has a high explosive proximity fused warhead which is lethal from 100 to more than 60,000 feet.

Should enemy aircraft elude both fighter screen and SAM area coverage, they would be attacked by the short-range missile batteries. Rapier has been in RAF Service since 1974 and is designed specifically to counter low flying aircraft. The three components of the system are the launcher, which houses a command link computer and antenna, a surveillance radar and IFF interrogator and four missile rounds. The second component is an optical tracker, the operator using a small joystick to hold the aiming mark on the centre of the aircraft. A TV tracker moving with the optical sight head measures missile deviation in flight and the computer generates correcting signals which are fed instantly to the missile from its command antenna in the launcher. The third element, a Marconi DN 181 Blindfire radar Tracker, generates a narrow radar beam which tracks both target and missile, feeding correction to the command guidance computer in the same way as the TV tracker of the optical system. The Marconi Tracker replaces the optical counterpart in poor visibility and at night, and is capable of detecting low flying aircraft at a range of 11.5 kilometres. British Aerospace, the manufacturer, claim a single shot kill probability of about 90 per cent with Blindfire and 75 per cent with the optical tracker.

Short-range air defence (SHORAD) is provided in Scotland by two RAF Regiment Squadrons, No 48 at Lossiemouth and No 27 at Leuchars. Both are mobile and would deploy away from their main base in time of crisis. A squadron usually comprises eight fire units, with a Sergeant detachment commander, a Corporal Second-in-Command and a team of six operators, reload parties and ground self

defence. Group Captain Buckley at Buchan had explained how the Rapier squadron could be integrated into an overall, continuously coordinated air defence net or they could, because of their comparatively short range, low level, ground defence responsibilities, operate autonomously within specified SHORAD zones. The author had watched No 48 Squadron gunners at Lossiemouth in the weapon simulator reacting within a 7–10 second decision time to high speed low level targets. Later, at Leuchars, he discussed Rapier crew training with WO Brendan Duffy, Squadron

That one is friendly: Rapier crew of No 48 Squadron RAF Regiment training at Lossiemouth (Author)

Warrant Officer on No 27 RAF Regiment Squadron who has spent many of his 26 years in the Regiment in air defence duties. He explained that after initial operator training at West Raynham, the operator would be assessed on his tracking abilities weekly and would have to meet very rigorous aircraft recognition standards. For example, with representations of an aircraft size and shape, in different light and at different angles at a simulated distance of 1 kilometre and 4 seconds, the operator had to achieve a 100 per cent friend or foe identification and a 90 per cent individual aircraft type recognition. Each operator had to pass a Categorisation Board three times a year and had to be proficient in routine equipment servicing, safety procedures, tactical driving, first aid and Nuclear, Chemical and Biological Warfare protection. The squadron, along with other RAF and Army Rapier squadrons, went regularly to the Hebrides range at Benbecula for live weapons training. WO Duffy also mentioned a deployment which was definitely not available for General Pile's soldiers in 1940: forward defensive commitments in NATO demanded periodic detachments to

Danish beaches in addition to the more widely publicised roulements to Belize.

The RAF Regiment is also responsible for low level defence in the Southern Sector, by Rapier squadrons and by providing the regular cadre in the two volunteer reserve Skyguard/ Oerlikon squadrons located in peacetime at RAF Waddington. No 1339 Wing, Royal Auxiliary Air Force Regiment, comprises No 2729 (City of Lincoln) and No 2890 Squadrons. It is commanded by a regular RAF Regiment officer, Wing Commander Mike Markey, whose Regiment service has taken him to many overseas areas and active duty in the Far East, Middle East and Northern Ireland. Typical of senior Regiment officers of his generation, he has commanded air defence, field and light armoured squadrons but, as he enthusiastically admits, he has not before commanded a unit with such unique characteristics as the Waddington RAAFR Wing.

The Skyguard radars and Oerlikon guns were captured from Argentine forces in the Falklands war, together with large quantities of ammunition. Skyguard can detect and track targets at 20 kilometres range. The system can track by radar or visually by TV. Identification of targets at ranges up to 12 kilometres is commonplace. The radar can control three Oerlikon 35mm calibre guns whose twin barrels can fire 550 rounds per minute per barrel. With three guns firing at a combined rate of 54 rounds per second, the kill probability is estimated to be between 90 and 100 per cent. The whole battery, including guns and radar is highly mobile, each gun is manned by a radar crew of three and a gun crew of four. With the exception of a regular RAF training and maintenance cadre, both squadrons are manned by civilian Auxiliaries who give up some weekends and one evening a week to participate in military training and associated outdoor pursuits such as adventure training, rock climbing, abseiling and skiing. The Auxiliaries are drawn from a wide range of civilian backgrounds. The Squadron Commander of No 2729 Squadron is head of sales with a defence optics firm. Airmen and airwomen include engineers, machinists, drivers,

Camouflaged Skyguard anti-aircraft radar of No 1339 Wing Royal Auxiliary Air Force Regiment at RAF Waddington *(No 1339 RAAFR Wing)*

and optician's assistant, a student nurse and an architect, with a wide age span drawn from both sexes.

In the composition of 1339 Wing there is a strong and reassuring echo of the Auxiliary Units in the Battle of Britain. Then, the best known reservists were the pilots of the 20 Auxiliary fighter squadrons called up on 24 August 1939. In November, No 607 (County of Durham) and 615 (County of Surrey) took their Gladiators across to France to support the British Expeditionary Force. By May 1940, 12 Auxiliary Squadrons, including 607 and 615, were equipped with either Hurricanes or Spitfires. One quarter of the squadrons appearing in the Fighter Command Order of Battle from July to October were initially Auxiliaries.

On 1 September, No 501 (County of Gloucester) Squadron began its third consecutive month in the heart of the battle at Biggin Hill. The following morning Pilot Officer A T Rose-Price reported for duty to his first Hurricane squadron. That afternoon 501 was scrambled with nine other squadrons of Hurricanes and Spitfires to meet an incoming raid of 250 aircraft over Kent.

The bulk of the ME 109 escorts were flying further from and well above the bomber stream and in addition to possessing numerical advantage of 2 to 1 they achieved tactical surprise. Four Hurricanes of 501 Squadron were shot down. One pilot escaped unhurt, two were wounded; Pilot Officer Rose-Price died on his first operational sortie. On 30 September, 501 Squadron was still in the front line, flying from Kenley, despite losing 16 more aircraft and five pilots during the month. The German victories had however been dearly bought. The most famous of 501's pilots, Sergeant J. H. (Ginger) Lacey had himself already shot down nine ME 109s and five other German aircraft.

In 1957, a Government Defence White Paper forecast the end of a manned bomber threat to Britain. As a result, the Auxiliary Squadrons were disbanded and the regular squadrons in Fighter Command drastically reduced. Regular fighter strength, if not numbers, has recovered, but the air defence legacy of Pilot Officer Rose-Price, Sergeant Lacey

One of the 35mm twin barrelled Oerlikon guns captured from the Argentines in the Falklands War, now equipping No 1339 Wing, Royal Auxiliary Air Force Regiment at Waddington *(No 1339 RAAFR Wing)*

and their many colleagues on the volunteer squadron named, like 2729 (City of Lincoln) Squadron for cities and counties of Britain, rests now on just two ground units at Waddington. The pride of Wing Commander Markey and his handful of regular airmen in their unusual inheritance is well placed.

The Groundcrews

In 1940 a fighter squadron comprised about 20 pilots, 20 fitters, 20 mechanics, five armourers, two or three senior NCOs and a couple of administrative clerks, to operate between 12 and 18 aircraft depending on the daily loss and replacement rate. There were usually two or three squadrons on each major airfield but deployments to forward bases were commonplace. In the critical days of late August and early September, the last fighter would return at dusk, after 9 pm, and be at readiness again six hours later. The squadron groundcrew worked shifts round the clock but, on many occasions surge rates during the day would prompt the recall to the line of those temporarily off duty. Where the airfields were hit, as increasingly occurred in that period, all hands were needed for rescue, firefighting and battle damage repairs.

In the second half of August, progressively more bombers got through and the airfields suffered increasing damage. Many scores of lives were saved by timely air raid warnings which allowed servicemen and women to take cover in shelters, but losses steadily mounted. Manston was repeatedly bombed. On the 18th, the sector operations rooms at Biggin Hill and Kenley were damaged with instant impact on the effectiveness of interceptions later in the day; a similar result occurred when North Weald operations room was severely damaged on 3 September. However, perhaps because the German bombers were dropping a high proportion of fragmentation bombs, designed to destroy parked aircraft, rather than high explosive, even some of the most concentrated attacks produced gratifyingly small casualty lists. There were tragic exceptions: on 30 August a WAAF shelter at Biggin Hill received a direct hit, with the loss of 39 lives. On some stations accumulated fatigue and frequent air attacks occasionally reduced

morale and groundcrew effectiveness, but these were exceptions. Individual feats of bravery were widespread: Sergeant Helen Turner and Corporal Elspeth Henderson were deservedly awarded the Military Medal for remaining at their Biggin Hill switchboard despite a direct hit on the Operations Room the day after so many of their colleagues had died on the same airfield. Maintenance, refuelling, battle repairs, arming, cooking: all went on amid unexploded bombs, fires, shattered buildings and, frequently, the unease caused by uncertainty about the fate of family in Portsmouth, or Rochester, or in any town in south-east England which could be victim of haphazard Luftwaffe bombing.

In 1990, there is no complacency in the RAF about the vulnerability of airfields to air attacks. Unless taxying for take-off or after landing, no fighters are visible on the ground. Instead, spread haphazardly across the airfield are hardened shelters (HAS), each housing one or two Phantoms or Tornadoes or up to four Hawks in their wartime deployment. Each HAS is linked to main taxiways and duplicated runways by more than one ribbon of concrete. In 1940 the consistently dry weather allowed the fighters to take off either from concrete runways or directly from the grass. A more usual British summer could have left the airfields too soft for even the relatively light weight Spitfires and Hurricanes, and too easily rutted for safe departures or landings. As a result, they too could be scattered about the airfield, some in revetments, some simply widely dispersed to reduce their vulnerability to air attack. Main hangars were used only when absolutely necessary for major servicing.

In 1940, the operations centres and CH stations were above ground and had little or no reinforcement. In 1990, the station operations room is heavily reinforced to standards akin to those of the HAS, both locations providing shelter for groundcrew. On the other hand, weapon technology has advanced considerably in the intervening years. The Ju 87 divebomber normally carried 4×110 lb bombs on its wing pylons; the Dornier 17 carried 2,200 lbs, the Ju 88 4,000 lbs. Bombs would either have a high explosive warhead designed to produce the maximum blast damage in a relatively small area, or fragmentation designed to spread

Testing for nerve gas: all part of the days work in Minival for General Mechanic SAC Andrew Porter at Leeming *(Author)*

smaller fragments over a wider area, particularly against parked aircraft. In 1990, free fall bombs would range from 250 to 1,000 lbs, but would be supplemented by air-to-ground missiles which, with various kinds of guidance, could be targetted against specific buildings or runways, or with unitary or submunition warheads against radio/radar emitters. Aircraft likely to be launched against British airfields could be carrying up to 15,000 lbs of weapons each.

As a result, all 11 Group fighter bases, in common with all other RAF stations, regularly hold exercises under circumstances simulating combat conditions as closely as possible. Some, imposed by RAF Strike Command, are without notice and known as Tactical Evaluations (TACEVALS), others organised by the stations themselves on a slightly smaller scale are derivatively referred to as MINIVALS. The scenarios and objectives for both are very similar: the airfield is directed to move to a fully manned war footing for an unspecified period and its ability to operate effectively while under 'attack' is examined.

At the end of November 1989, Group Captain John Rooum, Station and Force Commander of the Leeming Wing called a no notice MINIVAL. Within a very short time the War Operations Centre (WOC) was fully manned and Group Captain Rooum took his place on the 'Bridge' from where be could see a wide arc of wall displays illustrating the availability and readiness of all the major assets on his station.

Group Captain Rooum has been a fighter pilot throughout his service career, first on Lightnings, then Phantoms and now the Tornado F3, punctuating his 3,000 flying hours by the customary operations-related staff tours. He is typical of the RAF's front line station commanders: all with many hundreds of hours, usually on the aircraft flown on the base and always in the role discharged by the squadrons. The 11 Group station commanders are usually to be seen in flying suit and set high store on their professional credibility with their squadrons. Regular flying with the squadrons was a luxury denied to their predecessors in 1940, even if they were current on the Spitfire or Hurricane, which was very unlikely. Wing Commander Victor Beamish, commander of North Weald during the Battle was one honourable exception who earmarked a Hurricane for his own use, flew regularly in combat with the squadrons on his airfield and was accredited with two kills.

In war, the Station Commander, as Force Commander, would be on the ground but because he would also be current on the F3 or F4, he could fly combat missions if called upon to do so. His main responsibility, as Group Captain Rooum explained, is 'to provide armed aircraft to meet the task'. There is a standard NATO alert state which must be met: a proportion of his F3s at specific minutes readiness for scramble. In real crisis, he would receive constant readiness updates either directly or from Buchan SOC or Boulmer CRC. His peacetime task is to ensure that Leeming is prepared to respond. Once the war started, he would not interfere in the direct link between sector and aircrew unless problems occurred. The scramble procedure practised in isolation with the peacetime QRA fighters would be extended to all three Leeming squadrons.

If however, for some reason, a squadron could not meet its scramble times, or there were local reasons to switch resources between squadrons, he would have the information in front of him on which to make his decisions. At a glance, he can see the serviceability level of every aircraft, its readiness state and if relevant its airborne time, its crew and HAS location. On other displays he can see indicators of spares, weapons, fuel and other critical stores; major MT and ground equipment: ambulances, fuel bowsers, tractors; engineering facilities and manpower; resupply convoys to the HAS; surface-to-air defences, ground defences, battle damage including runway repair: all constantly updated to ensure that any problem likely to interfere with the responsiveness of the Leeming Wing is anticipated and dealt with.

Meanwhile his deputy, OC Operations Wing in peacetime, will be occupying an alternative operations centre elsewhere in the base. In most exercises, some reason is simulated to neutralise the WOC for a time and the alternative brought on line. This is slightly different from the circumstances at Kenley on 18 August 1940 when communications to the Operations Centre were severed and the entire staff had to move off base to a local shop where the GPO tapped the RAF lines into the local net.

Adjacent to the Force Commander in the Leeming WOC is the Ground Defence Commander, better known as OC Admin Wing and, in November 1989, Wing Commander Tim Pink of the Administrative Branch. His responsibility in war is to ensure that the base can survive and operate despite attack by air and on land. There is a close parallel between the possible threats to airfields in 1940 and 1990, despite the changes in the overall strategic environment. In any examination of the Battle of Britain, with a natural concentration on the fighting between the two air forces, it is easy to forget that there was a widely held belief that the country was in imminent danger of an invasion which would be spearheaded by parachute troops. There was no hindsight at the beginning of September, no awareness of German strategic uncertainty. The ringing of church bells was to be the signal for the arrival of the enemy. Consequently, all the major airfields were guarded by infantry as well as by the batteries of Anti-Aircraft Command.

In 1990 a recognised element in the threat to the United Kingdom air bases, and especially to those located near the east coast, lies in the special forces of the Soviet Union trained in behind-the-lines operations, including attacks

Mobile reaction force on exercise at RAF Leeming *(Author)*

on airfields. Now, however, all ground defence is provided from within the station's own resources. During this particular exercise for example, a four man patrol, known as a Squadron Mobile Reaction Force, was led by Corporal Ian Stewart, an airframe technician from No 25 Squadron. His wartime routine would comprise a 12 hour maintenance shift on the squadron, a four hour guard duty and, hopefully, eight hours rest. As in 1940 his 'rest' period would not necessarily be observed by the opposition and he would be recalled for his trade duties whenever required. The task of his patrol was to spot unexploded bombs and look out for any intruders: in short to keep his site clear for aircraft movement. All his patrol were trained in the use of the automatic weapons which they carried.

Inside the WOC, by 1700 on the second day of the MINIVAL, the Ground Defence Commander and his team were busy. On the large scale station ground plan covering the display wall, Wing Commander Pink described the extent of the 'damage' inflicted by an 'air attack' which had penetrated the fighter defences a few minutes previously. The 'attackers' had in fact been four enthusiastically flown Tornado GR 1s whose high speed low level pass over the base had added to a sense of realism already high with groundcrew wearing their nuclear, chemical and biological (NBC) protective clothing and carrying sidearms.

Wing Commander Pink pointed out the locations of several identified unexploded bombs, craters on a taxi way and access road within the HAS site, another cutting a main traffic route and others on the main runway. Fortunately, there was still enough runway left intact to allow the F3s to launch and recover. The bulk fuel installations and ground equipment hangars were on fire, the tyre store had been destroyed and the engine repair bay damaged. Details of all damage were being rapidly plotted so that the Force Commander, with counsel from OC Engineering Wing and the Ground Defence Commander, could determine priorities for clearance.

Plotting the 'bomb damage' in the War Operations Centre at Leeming *(Author)*

One officer standing comparatively aloof from the activity was the station ground defence training officer, Flight Lieutenant Gareth Jones. He had devised much of the exercise scenario, trained the ground defence teams and was now impartially seeking to assess both the reality of the scenario and the effectiveness of his training. As there were plenty of opportunities for individual initiative by both defenders and 'intruders' – including seizure of control of the internal station tannoy system for 'spoof' messages, it was quite obvious that much was being learned on all sides.

In the exercise, as in war, some of the station staff simply extended their normal activities to round the clock shifts: the engineer and supply staff for example. Others, such as the officers and SNCOs of Administrative Wing, led by Wing Commander Pink, abandoned their personnel, accounts and education offices to become active defence commanders or passive defence controllers. Their activities were the direct legacy of the lessons learned at Hawkinge, Gravesend, Hornchurch, Rochester, Eastchurch, Kenley, Biggin Hill, North Weald, Manston and many other airfields in 1940. The aircrew, as always, would fight the enemy in the air but now all groundcrew would be prepared for personal combat on and around the airfield. Ironically, while females are not allowed to fly combat aircraft, they lead and participate in armed patrols on the ground. The modern TACEVAL or MINIVAL exercises only last a few days, not the incessant months of the Battle of Britain. They are, however, a regular reminder of the price of constant combat readiness and of the strain which continuous 24 hour operations can impose upon groundcrew and aircrew alike, even without the additional pressure of real combat fatigue. They are also a reminder, if such were needed, that modern airbases are so operationally important that casualties are unlikely to be confined to aircrew.

In day to day groundcrew activities, an airman or Ground Branch officer from 1940 would quickly be at home in the general structure of ground support but he would probably be startled by the impact of modern technology. The unbroken circle of ground support begins when the Tornado touches down after a safe recovery by Air Traffic Control and the flight line mechanics or HAS crew place the external ladder up to the cockpit. The circle ends when the processes are reversed. In between are the squadron first line maintenance technicians, the deeper engineering support of Engineering Wing, and, enveloping the whole with feeding, housing, paying, training, health and military security, the staffs of Administrative Wing.

An overall watching brief on engineering activities in 11 Group is maintained on behalf of the AOC by Group Captain Rod Brumpton at Bentley Priory. He was in no doubt about the most significant change in engineering practices since he himself joined the RAF as a Cranwell cadet in 1967. 'It is the emphasis on "high tech". Even the youngest mechanics and technicians must be at least computer literate; more senior airmen must learn to adapt their previous training and background.'

If 11 Group represents one end of the engineering chain of support, the other lies in the squadrons. Instantly recognisable to an airman or airwoman in 1940 or 1990 is the Squadron Warrant Officer: the day to day leader of the groundcrew and manager of their resources, reporting through the Squadron Engineering Officer to the Squadron Com-

A practical problem: how to cope with field rations while wearing NBC kit *(Sgt Steve Allsopp)*

mander. Warrant Officer Jack Berry of 43 Squadron joined the RAF as a Halton Apprentice in 1960 and has spent the last eight years working on Tornadoes. At the beginning of 1990, 43 Squadron was in the process of converting from the Phantom to the Tornado, and just as the aircrew were being called upon to cross an operational generation gap so, in WO Berry's words, 'There is a massive jump in avionics and engines from the F4 to the F3. The groundcrew need a much greater understanding of electronics and how a computer works. Many do a lead-in course now at Cosford on basic computers.'

Oddly enough, the second change in operating environment emphasised by WO Berry would not have surprised his Battle of Britain predecessors. With the Hurricanes and Spitfires dispersed for safety around the airfield, routine turn rounds and first time servicing was completed as far as possible out in the open. Hangars were obvious and vulnerable targets, to be avoided wherever possible. In the years of peace after the Second World War, and before the Soviet Air Force acquired its current radius of action, the threat of airfield attack diminished. It was not uncommon to see neat lines of fighters drawn up in front of the squadron hangar ready for take off. Unless the

Non destructive testing check by Sgt R Parkin at RAF Chivenor *(Cpl G Iverson ABiPP)*

squadron was night flying, the planes would be towed back into the hangar at dusk for maintenance as required by the late shift.

Then, in June 1967, the world was given a sharp reminder that airfields did not just launch air attacks; they could be on the receiving end as well; as the Israeli Air Force decimated neat rows of Egyptian, Syrian and Jordanian aircraft and then destroyed their hangars for good measure. The date coincided with a major re-equipment programme in the Soviet Air Force and the lesson was not lost on the RAF and our NATO allies. In 1990, the fighters are again sensibly dispersed around the airfields, but now in bombproof shelters. WO Berry described how much greater responsibility devolved upon his corporals in charge of each HAS handling team: three men for routine aircraft turn-round, supplemented as required for first line maintenance by a mobile team from the squadron. As a result, the corporals had broader demands on their trade knowledge, experience and leadership, while senior supervision was more complicated, especially in an exercise environment.

The story was developed further at Leeming by one such Corporal, Ian Shucksmith, on 25 Squadron in his first tour in rank after 5½ years service. He was responsible for the operational turn-round (OTR) in the HAS and ensuring that his two Tornadoes were armed and fuelled, with all routine servicing complete and any more major faults notified to his SNCO who could be either in the Squadron HQ HAS or in one of the others in the 25 Squadron area. In war, he would work a 12 hour shift in the HAS, which has its own heating and fume extraction systems, and then return to the hardened squadron personnel shelter to sleep, or to take his turn on guard duties.

In fighter operations it is invidious to identify any one supporting activity as more crucial than others, but the speed and efficiency of an OTR obviously determines the time an aircraft spends out of action on the ground. In 1980, British Aerospace presented the Skyflash Trophy to the RAF, for competition by OTR teams in 11 Group. In the competition, wartime circumstances are simulated as far as possible, with an aircraft assumed to have just landed after a combat sortie. The team wear respir-

ator, NBC suit and heavy gloves as they change
the brake parachute, replenish oil and fuel and
re-arm with four Skyflash, four AIM 9 missiles
and either 1100 Vulcan rounds or 160 Mauser
rounds of ammunition, depending on whether
the aircraft is a Phantom or Tornado. The
aircraft is assumed to have jettisoned its
underwing fuel tanks and these also have to be
replaced. To win the competition, the crew
know that their aircraft must be ready for
launching in well under an hour. The competition is designed to identify the best OTR team
in 11 Group, to stimulate improvement in
OTR standards, to provide opportunities for
possible improvement in OTR schedules and
to stress the importance of leadership and
decision-making by the NCOs in charge of the
teams. Not surprisingly, the Trophy is widely
coveted and is held in 1990 with considerable
satisfaction by the groundcrew of 111 Squadron at Leuchars.

Sky flash and AIM 9 missiles at readiness in a HAS
at RAF Wattisham *(Sgt Steve Allsopp)*

A number of missiles are stored in the HAS
with the aircraft but, as in 1940, they would be
replenished from a weapon store located
elsewhere on the airfield. At Leeming, the
Explosives Support Flight, within Engineering
Wing, looks after the Skyflash and AIM 9
missiles, and the 27mm ammunition for the
Tornado's Mauser cannon. The missiles are
assembled in the flight from components and
then stripped down periodically to ensure that
no deterioration has occurred in storage. When
a missile has been exposed to the environment,
when for example it has been carried by the
QRA aircraft, it will be returned after a shorter
period for inspection and reassembly.

Flight Lieutenant Andy Madge commands
50 radar and armament tradesmen. Whereas
his predecessors in 1940 were simply concerned with bullets and cannon shells, his
radar tradesmen maintain the forebody of the
Skyflash and the guidance and combat system
of the AIM 9, while his armourers are specialist
missile technicians. Skyflash is a medium
range missile which is guided to its target by the
F3's illuminating radar, with a proximity fuse
which activates a high explosive fragmentation
warhead at the correct distance. The short
range AIM 9, on the other hand, is fired by the
Tornado within radar aligned parameters and
then, by a seeker in the missile head, homes on
to the heat generated by engines or airframe

structures of the target aircraft. The 27mm
Mauser cannon is fitted in a fuselage tank and
presents the armourers with more traditional
tasks of ammunition storage and weapon
maintenance.

The range and depth of trade skills demanded by the Tornado F3 can be indicated by a
brief survey of its avionic and aerodynamic
systems, compared to the rudimentary instruments, controls and construction of the first
generation monoplane Hurricanes and
Spitfires. In the nose is the AI24 Foxhunter
Radar, the F3's primary sensor, with state of
the art microwave systems, digital circuits, data
handling technology and integrated ECM.
Communications include a secure, spread
spectrum ECM resistent data link; HF, VHF
and UHF radios; tape recorders; defensive
threat warning systems with automatic chaff
and flare dispensers. Other avionics include
Tactical Air Navigation (TACAN) and Instru-
mental Landing System (ILS); electronic
head-down and pilot head-up displays; a main
computer incorporating flight planning and
navigation; cathode ray displays, computerised
and manual fire control systems. The aircraft's
flying controls are all electrical, 'flying by wire'
with electrical and mechanical backup modes:
the first Royal Air Force squadron aircraft with
such features. The system comprises three sets

Left: Major servicing. A Phantom of No 56 Squadron at Wattisham *(Sgt Steve Allsopp)*
Below: SACW Elisabeth Blanchard and Cpl Malcolm Earl replacing the spine panel of an F4 of No 56 Squadron *(Author)*

of triplicated rate gyros and two computers. A further computer in the flying control system automatically prevents the pilot taking the aircraft into a spin when manoeuvring in close combat. Further systems operate the automatic wing sweep. Each of the two RB 99 three spool, reheated turbofan engines have digital, automatic controls which secure optimum operating conditions according to throttle demands. Most aircraft systems have built in test equipment which gives groundcrew and aircrew rapid indication of faults, many of which can be rectified by replacement units on the flight line. Not surprisingly therefore the days of groundcrew classification simply by 'rigger', or 'electrical' are long past. Now many different trades, with specialist 'Q' equipment qualifications are required to ensure that the modern fighter can be kept serviceable.

Therein lies a further difference from the Hurricane and Spitfire days. Now, with greater use made of replaceable units on the flight line and automatic fault diagnosis, the technician on the first line may actually need less technical expertise than his predecessors, while his colleagues back across the airfield in Engineering Wing will certainly need much more.

Wing Commander Chris Hockley, who runs the Engineering and Supply Wing at Watisham, considers that the Phantom is 'fairly simple' when compared with the F3. To the non-specialist observer, his comparison is certainly 'relative'. Whereas the squadron engineers are responding to maintenance

requirements as they occur, Wing Commander Hockley's task, like his colleagues on the F3 wings, is to provide periodic deeper servicing at three different levels. He compared his timetable with that of the car owner who puts his car in for regular servicing as recommended by the manufacturers: with a principle of deeper examination and component replacement taking place over longer intervals. This is an obvious difference from the operating circumstances of 1940, when normal wear and tear, or 'mean time between failure rates', or whole life deterioration of components, were almost without exception overtaken by combat loss or damage. 'Scheduled servicing' would have been a luxury to be appreciated then.

Now however, both efficient maintenance and economic resource allocation demand, in peacetime, carefully planned and managed rectification programmes. For example, after every 1,000 flying hours the Phantom will be brought into Engineering Wing for a 35 day deep inspection and component replacement: engines; hydraulic components, flaps and all areas of the airframe and major systems involving the removal of 200 'doors' or panels in checking for incipient structural problems. Modern combat training imposes metal fatigue which is constantly monitored and, as the Phantoms move well along their forecast in-service life span, the airframe technicians in particular are kept at full stretch. They will usually be corporals or junior technicians with up to 10 years experience on the Phantom. They will not have the modern built-in test equipment available to their colleagues working on the Tornadoes and consequently rely heavily on their accumulated experience and extensive training.

Elsewhere in Engineering and Supply Wing, squadrons or flights concentrate specialist expertise on engines, hydraulic systems, avionics, electronics and radars as well as providing engineering support for Air Traffic Control communications and radars, ground equipment, MT and the supply of all aircraft spare parts and domestic items. A sign of the times is the renaming of the 'Ground Radio Flight' to 'Communications and Information Systems Engineering Flight'. Computer processing and data links now contribute to many traditional station activities. Personnel records, stocks, engineering schedules have all been transferred to computer data bases, and the men and women of CIS-Eng Flight have had to extend their maintenance expertise accordingly. Altogether, Wing Commander Hockley commands 690 airmen and air women; a smaller number than his colleagues on the Tornado bases because they all have either more aircraft or additional training units or both.

The engineering progression from Phantom to Tornado is marked, but incomparable to the step from servicing the Shackleton, with its roots in Second World War technology, to the maintenance of the mission systems of the E3 Sentry. The groundcrew on 8 Squadron at Lossiemouth obviously regarded their 'Shack' with the same mixture of affection and occasional exasperation as their aircrew colleagues. Sergeant Chris Earley for example had previously spent three years on the Tornado at

Engineering management: computer assisted. Warrant Officer Malcolm Simpson: Engineering Coordinator at RAF Wattisham *(Author)*

Boscombe Down and found himself employing engineering skills which he hadn't used since his basic training in 1974: cutting threads, replacing studs and generally taking apart and rebuilding engines in a manner reminiscent of a Spitfire engine fitter. 'There is,' he said, 'a great job satisfaction in making the repair than simply replacing a black box, but it takes a lot of time.' Corporal Craig McKinlay had previously worked on Harriers. 'The APS 20', he explained 'differs from modern radars. It has a lot of parts bolted on and has both the original valves and digital equipment for signal enhancement and decoding, providing a lot of problems but a lot of job satisfaction.' Corporal Alix Wilcox, as an airframe technician, dealt with the most obvious Shackleton problem areas: an old aircraft, constantly exposed to a maritime environment, with engine panels, spars and frame vulnerable to corrosion and cracking. Flying controls had to be replaced and getting spare parts could be very difficult. He shared the view of his two colleagues: 'A lot of job satisfaction, but a lot of hours needed to keep the aircraft flying; yes, I would like to go on now to a new aircraft and new equipment.' No greater contrast could be found than in Mission Support Wing (MSW) Waddington, where the groundcrew are almost entirely computer specialists, or computer trained, to provide the backup for the E3D Sentry.

Commanded by Wing Commander Ken Pilbeam, an ex-V Force and Electronic Warfare specialist AEO, MSW has three squadrons whose responsibilities can be swiftly summarised but whose content masks a major departure from traditional RAF practices. The

Sentry AWACS mission system is entirely computer based and relies on video maps, aircraft performance data, navigational detail, and specialist mission data on magnetic tapes. The E3D has six times the computer capacity of the earlier equipment on board the USAF and NATO E3A. At least 50 tapes are required for each sortie and Wing Commander Pilbeam envisages that MSW will ultimately build up a data bank of 12,000 tapes.

The task of the Software Data Squadron commanded by Squadron Leader Bob Ford is to prepare and update tapes for each sortie, record the tapes post flight for analysis and progressively develop the software to modify the aircraft mission systems in line with changing operational circumstances and threat assessment. The Automatic Data Processing and Support Squadron is responsible for the security and maintenance of the mainframe computer and all hardware and tapes associated with it. Squadron Leader John Faiers, the Squadron Commander, explained how the main operational programme for each sortie carried all the data base for the management of all the aircraft's sensors. The aircraft itself on each sortie will produce a lot of information which had to be passed to other agencies after reduction to a manageable form. Software was needed for all the ancillary programmes and visual display units. The complete dependence of the E3D on computer systems demanded

Ultra Modern Simulation: The 'cockpit' of the E3D Sentry at Waddington
(Rediffusion Simulation)

fully integrated software and hardware support with secure and available storage of data 365 days a year, 24 hours a day.

The third squadron operates two simulators, one for the flight deck crews and one for the mission crew. The former, the 'Dynamic' simulator is a direct descendant, albeit many generations removed, of the Link trainer familiar to 1940's aircrew. The Link was a rudimentary cockpit which introduced the pilot to the interaction between basic controls and flying surface. The E3 Dynamic Simulator is a multi-million dollar reproduction of the Sentry's flight deck in every detail. Pilot, Co-Pilot and Flight Engineers can 'fly' complete sorties and be presented by either the simulator operator or programmed tapes with every conceivable E3D position from routine cruise with all systems working to multiple emergencies at the most difficult phases of landing and take off. Such simulations are now common to many phases of combat flying, but not with the degree of sophistication of the E3D. Originally, the simulator was seen, like the Link, as a valuable initial training aid. Now it is regarded as an integral element of continuation training. The crews of the newly constituted 8 Squadron can expect to fly approximately three 3-hour 'sorties' on the simulator each month.

The Mission Simulator is even more complex, as it replicates nine mission crew positions. Ultimately it will use exactly the same computer tape as the real aircraft and crews will fly a number of 'missions' which will range from area scenarios lasting five hours or more to specific continuation training on practice intercepts and tracking.

Within Engineering Wing is the Sentry AEW Maintenance School whose trainee ground technicians will also cut their teeth on the Mission Simulator as they learn Sentry systems maintenance, operating and fault finding. Snatches of conversation with three of the senior NCOs who are training the Sentry's ground crew illustrate the extent of the aircraft's dependence on computer based systems. Chief Technician Mick Hall, air radar technician: 'The mission system radar will interface with the main computer and IFF . . . . The digital doppler processor gives track, range and velocity information . . . . Radar data computers will put target reports together, pass them to the main computer which transfers the data to displays . . . 90 per cent of faults will be automatically corrected by the switch in of replacement units . . . .' Flight Sergeant Dennis Smith, Flight Systems Technician: 'It is a modular computer concept, the Display Technician can replace circuit boards very easily during flight . . . . The Electronic Support Measures equipment is new to the E3D, the earlier AEW aircraft don't have it, so we shall need to work out the interface with the computer . . . .' Flight Sergeant Duncan Colville, Air Engineer Technician: 'It is basically a traditional airframe, but the high by-pass turbo-fan engines are a big step forward, being much more efficient and, located in pods, much more accessible . . . . Down the back we shall need ex Cosford specialists: the whole thing requires computer awareness far more than Nimrod and Tornado.'

Mission Support Wing at Waddington is a long way from half a dozen fitters, armourers and riggers tumbling out of the back of a lorry to patch up the Hurricanes ready for first light the following morning; groping for the spanners, replacing the plugs, replaiting the wiring, soldering the broken switches or replacing shattered links to the ailerons – all in the increasingly chill autumn night air with the Flight Sergeant constantly shouting reminders about the Blackout when paraffin lamps seemed to give more light over a hundred yards than they did over three feet.

The following morning however, the Hurricane pilots were dependent on procedures which Sentry aircrew would recognise instantly: the procedures which ensure that the combat aircraft leave, and safely return to their airfields; the most visible link between ground support and air operations: Air Traffic Control. At least, the take off procedures would be similar, with Air Traffic giving barometric settings for altimeters, runway or grass field take off direction, taxi and take off clearances, and hand over when airborne to the controlling agency. Recovery to the airfield however could be very different. In 1940, bad weather and low cloud could present a greater hazard than battle damage because, provided flying control was retained, the low speed and short landing run required by both Spitfire and Hurricane allowed many pilots to escape unhurt from forced landings away from base. In 1990, the threshold speed of a Phantom or Tornado could be in excess of 120 knots and several hundred yards of reinforced concrete are required to carry the landing weight of either. The alternative to an airfield landing is ejection. On the other hand the hazards of bad weather, except for very high runway crosswinds, have been greatly reduced by ground approach radar and on-board instrument landing systems. The approach controller in the tower will talk down the pilot to a height of 1,500 feet 10 miles from the runway; thereafter he will be brought down to the runway threshold or to visual sighting of it, by the ATC radar director. If the pilot should lose his R/T he will be given clearance to land by Verey pistol flares: a procedure unchanged over the years.

When the Hurricane and Spitfire pilot recovered to their airfields they kept a sharp lookout for colleagues in the circuit and for free hunting ME 109s. Now, particularly over the more southerly fighter bases, there is the modern hazard of civilian light aircraft. For example, light aircraft movements through the airspace controlled by RAF Wattisham have doubled in less than two years. Indeed, civilian traffic in many parts of the UKADR is so heavy that joint civil military control is exercised from common user regional air traffic centres. Communications are so well coordinated that one agency, the Distress and Diversion cell at West Drayton could in peacetime take executive control of any aircraft in an emergency from either local air traffic or the regional centres. The regional centres in turn feed in details of civilian traffic to the radar Control and Reporting Centres and Posts, thus completing the air-to-ground and ground-to-air control and communication links.

All the groundwork in 11 Group is designed to ensure that the Tornadoes and Phantoms, with their crews, are fully prepared for their next sorties. Once airborne they will depend to a great extent on fighter controllers to position them in the right place at the right time. They will recover to their airfields, or to diversion airfields, with the assistance of the air traffic controllers. Once there, the ground tradesmen and women and ground branch officers will continue the cycle which was first proven in the high summer and early autumn of 1940.

Chapter Seven

UNITED
WE STAND

B Y JULY 1940 Britain had lost her allies in Europe. Her friends and kin in the Commonwealth were too far away and too unprepared themselves to send speedy assistance, although by 1945 strong support had been received from Canada, Rhodesia, South Africa, Australia, New Zealand and several other countries still governed by Britain. The United States Government under President Roosevelt was sympathetic but facing strong domestic opposition to any move to become involved in the European war. The Soviet Union had signed a non-aggression treaty with Germany in 1939 and very few people in Britain in 1940 anticipated that an Anglo-Soviet alliance was less than 12 months away. Britain's fate was to rest in her own hands and those of a handful of brave and adventurous men who had managed to escape from their homelands in Europe or travelled as individual volunteers from several countries in the Commonwealth to fly and fight in the Royal Air Force.

In 1940, large numbers of Poles and Czechs escaped to Britain, among them many fighter pilots. Some had come to Britain via the French Foreign Legion and *L'Armée de L'Air*. Some Czech navigators, on finding that onward transfer to the French Air Force from the Foreign Legion was only available to pilots, instantly lost their log books and were occasionally a little erratic when they subsequently 'converted' on to new types of single seat fighter. At first the emigrés were absorbed into existing fighter squadrons but as their numbers grew both the Poles and Czechs formed indigenous units. No 302 (City of Poznan) formed on 17 July and No 303 (Kosciuszko) Squadron on 2 August. Before the end of the month, No 310 (Czechoslovak) Squadron was flying Hurricanes from Duxford and in September No 312 (Czechoslovak) Squadron began operations at Speke, also with Hurricanes. By the end of the Battle, 300 Czech, Polish, French and Belgian pilots had fought and many had died, including Sergeant Josef Frantisek of 303 Squadron who with 17 kills, all in September, was the joint RAF top scorer of the Battle.

The Commonwealth pilots usually flew with British squadrons but, at the end of June, No 1 Royal Canadian Air Force Squadron began to form with Hurricanes at Middle Wallop. It subsequently moved to the heart of the Battle at Croydon and later to Northolt. Seven American pilots flew with RAF squadrons before the formation on 19 September of No 71 (Eagle) Squadron at Church Fenton. The first, Pilot Officer Billy Fiske, joined 601 Squadron at Tangmere on 15 July. He was also the first to give his life when a month later he landed his damaged Hurricane back at Tangmere just as the airfield was being heavily attacked by Ju 87s. His aircraft was hit and caught fire. Although rescued from his cockpit, he died subsequently from his burns. Of the other six, four were posted to Church Fenton in September to form the nucleus of No 71 Squadron. Sadly, only one, Flying Officer J K Haviland DFC, survived the war.

In 1990 Britain's defence is anchored firmly in the NATO alliance. Ground forces are deployed in central Europe in an allied command structure. The Royal Navy is closely

91

integrated within NATO's maritime Commands of Atlantic and Channel. The Commander-in-Chief of Royal Air Force Strike Command, Air Chief Marshal Sir Patrick Hine, is also C-in-C UK Air, a major command within the overall NATO responsibilities of Supreme Allied Commander Europe. In addition there are more than two dozen NATO officers on exchange duties within 11 Group alone, as well as a sprinkling of Australians and New Zealanders.

In 1990, the allied and commonwealth 'exchange' officers in 11 Group are still all volunteers, but none of them required flying training, or indeed any other kind of professional training other than, in some cases, conversion to type. As a result, they all bring a considerable amount of experience of different kinds to enhance their temporary British environment. Among them are squadron pilots and navigators, instructor pilots at the TWUs, pilots and navigators at the OCUs, fighter controllers, air traffic controllers, AEW specialists and engineers.

The following pen pictures of some of the exchange officers in 11 Group in 1990 illustrate just how great is the aggregate of the experience which they contribute.

Lieutenant Bryan 'Spot' Kust is a United States Navy pilot now flying the Tornado F3 as a staff member of No 229 OCU. His previous assignment had been with USN VF 213 Squadron on board USS *Enterprise*, flying F14 Tomcats on which he had accumulated 900 hours. He had flown CAPs off the Libyan coast and provided top cover for attack operations in the Gulf in 1988. He was obviously finding activities at Coningsby not quite so hectic as on board Enterprise: 'You could feel the tension on the deck with 60 to 70 aircraft, propellors spinning, weapons, cables everywhere. When doing pre-flight checks on the back of the F14 you had to be careful not to slip and fall overboard.' He was clearly enjoying the big wide open and static spaces at Coningsby.

Lieutenant Kust's partner at Coningsby is navigator Lieutenant Evan Edwards, an Annapolis graduate of 1983 who, since training, has flown nothing but the F14 Tomcat. He had found much in common with F3 operations: combined efforts between pilot and navigator were essential and an F14 navigator would fly with the same pilot for most of the time. Lieutenant Edwards was clearly not missing the critical time at catapult launch, when if pressure is low or the catapult fails, the Tomcat crew would have about a second to react before they are over the bow and their parachutes are dragging towards the ship's propellors. He would leave his OCU students in no doubt about the operational need for precise navigation, and not just because his previous 'airfield' could have moved 20 miles away before he returned, but also because a specific flight profile in war could be a factor in IFF. Like all F14 crews, he was familiar with working with AEW and tactics were generally similar. Like most of his USAF colleagues, he was finding the RAF's commitment to low flying an interesting and novel experience.

Captain Jim Galloway USAF is an F3 pilot with 23 Squadron at Leeming. He brings the experience of 1,650 fighter hours, of which the previous 800 had been on the F15 as an instructor pilot at Tyndall Air Force Base (AFB) in Florida and with 27 Squadron at Langley AFB Virginia. He was very familiar with the QRA responsibilities of 11 Group after fulfilling similar duties round the clock off the United States east coast, when Soviet Air Force aircraft were either transitting to or probing from bases in Cuba. Captain Galloway had also flown sorties in support of United States Government drug enforcement agencies. Like his F14 colleagues he commented on the RAF's different emphasis on low level flying. The F15 crews train to 1,000 feet, then on their squadron down to 500 feet, and exceptionally to 300 feet. Here he was down to 250 feet as a matter of course.

Captain Brad Dolan is on exchange from the Royal Canadian Air Force with 29 Squadron at Coningsby and brings the experience of 1,000 hours on the CF18 out of a total of 3,000 as a fighter pilot. Despite his experience, and similarities between Tornado air defence operations and those of the CF18 and earlier CF101, he had observed that in some areas there was a sharper operational environment to 11 Group. He attributed this to working out of the HAS, to operating a great deal out over the sea and to the vagaries of British weather: 'Your island can't steam into wind!' As he described it, an exchange pilot received no favours from his hosts; his day was exactly the same as theirs. A standard 'fourship' exercise would be preceded by the usual briefings on 'met', maintenance, routeing, emergencies and intelligence and specific sortie details of frequencies, call-signs and other agencies e.g. ground control and tankers. Tactical briefing would be much shorter than those at the OCU; perhaps a reference to 'SOPs', for 'Standard Operational Procedures', perhaps a note on how to mount the CAP station to leave as much time as possible for tactics. Then on with the G suit and immersion suit which takes about 10 minutes, detailed check out at the Squadron 'ops' desk; in peacetime, walk or hitch a ride across to the relevant HAS and prepare for takeoff. The two pairs are usually separated by 1,000 feet during takeoff and radar contact is maintained between them as they head out to the CAP area. Captain Dolan emphasised the need to keep a sharp lookout in British airspace, especially when not under SOC control. A normal training sortie would last for 1½ hours, with the Tornadoes taking it in turns to be the aggressors and the pair on CAP. A tanker rendezvous is usually arranged beforehand, and while one pair is refuelling, the other will do a one-to-one practice interception between them. Captain Dolan had only joined 29 Squadron in August 1989 and was still theoretically a junior pilot, but the familiarity with air defence operations bred from his previous 3,000 hours was obvious.

Captain Bruno Jovet of the French Air Force was about to join 29 Squadron at Coningsby after 1,200 hours on the Mirage FIC and Mirage 2000. His squadron at Orange, No 15 (Vendée) had the greatest number of victories in the French Air Force since its formation in the First World War. He had flown in Chad as part of the French intervention force but the greater part of his experience had been in the French air defence environment. Because of a different geographical scenario, French fighters do not mount CAPs but scramble from ground alert. The Mirage 2000 climbs to 50,000 feet at Mach 2 but has a shorter endurance than the Tornado. Captain Jovet had participated in many NATO exercises and was well prepared for interceptions with UK ground and AEW control.

NATO Multinational E3 *(Sqn Ldr T R Paxton)*

Captain Kai Nergaard of the Royal Norwegian Air Force was about to join No 11 Squadron. As an ex F5 and F16 pilot, trained to fire shorter range AIM 9 missiles and guns he had brought a very different kind of air defence expertise to 11 Group. His experience would be invaluable on the many occasions out over the North Sea when the Tornado squadrons were working closely with their Norwegian allies.

The changed shape of British defence interests over the last 50 years is reflected in the presence of only two Australian exchange officers in 11 Group. Flight Lieutenant Jim Eaglen flew Mirage III multi-role aircraft with the RAAF and has a total of 1,500 flying hours. The difference in threat assessment in the two hemispheres is marked by the fact that Flight Lieutenant Eaglen has done more night flying on 5 Squadron in one year than in the previous four on the Mirage III. He had also noted the associated differences in the operational ground environment, with the realistic simulation in exercises of likely circumstances in war.

Away from the front line is Captain Jay Patenaude USAF, a weapons controller instructor on the E3D Training Squadron at Waddington. Prior to his assessment in 11 Group, he was a weapons director with the 552nd Airborne Warning and Control Wing at Tinker AFB in Oklahoma. The experience of an officer such as Captain Patenaude is invaluable to the RAF as it prepares to introduce its own variant of the USAF's AWACs. British crews have trained with the NATO E3s and No 8 Squadron has worked for several years alongside its USAF counterparts. As weapons controller in the AWACs team, Captain Patenaude's duties resemble those of the intercept controller on the ground. Should a SOC be unable to maintain control, the AEW aircraft would assume responsibilities for scrambling fighters, assigning CAPs and controlling fighters to intercept positions after locating its incoming raids. In Captain Patenaude, in his training position, there is direct access for the 'ab initio' British weapons controllers to draw directly on 12 years of USAF operational experience.

Among all the exchange officers, none represent the realignment of British air defence more than Hauptmann Detleff Gosda and his navigator Hauptmann Armin Gross, a Phantom crew on 56 Squadron at Wattisham. Hauptmann Gosda came from No 36 fighter-bomber Wing at Hopsten in the Federal Republic of Germany, while Hauptmann Gross flew with No 71 (*Richtofen*) Wing at Wittmundhafen. Both are experienced F4 aircrew, with 1,250 and 1,350 hours respectively on the aircraft. Although the German Phantom F4F is similar to the FGR2 flown by 56 Squadron, it does not have a pulse-doppler AI radar and is equipped only with AIM 9 missiles and guns. Hauptmann Gosda expressed great satisfaction at flying more frequently with 56 than he had done back at home. Such is the natural acceptance of the German crews in a British fighter squadron that apart from the occasional leg-pull – by either side – the incongruity of Luftwaffe aircrew sharing in the Royal Air Force legacy of 1940 is not even a topic of conversation. Indeed when one reflects on the skills demonstrated by Hauptmann Gosda and Gross's illustrious predecessors, and maintained by the air force of the Federal Republic in 1990, the combination of both air forces presents a formidable proposition to any would be aggressor.

However, valuable as the presence of exchange officers is to the breadth and depth of 11 Group's operational effectiveness, it is the coordination of air defence assets in the Alliance which marks the biggest single difference in Britain's position in 1990 from that of

1940. The eastern boundary of the UKADR joins, running north to south, the Norwegian Air Defences, under overall command in war of Commander-in-Chief Air Forces Northern Europe, the Danish Air Force, under Commander Air Forces Baltic Approaches, the West German, Dutch and Belgian Air Forces, under Commander-in-Chief Second Tactical Air Force, and the French national Air Defence region. In time of crisis, the whole would be reinforced by 1,500 USAF fighters from the north American continent plus aircraft embarked on USN aircraft carriers deployed in European waters.

All coordination is tightly knit, but cooperation between 11 Group and the Norwegian and Danish air defences is particularly close. Norwegian F16s mount QRA readiness states in a similar manner to the 11 Group squadrons, as the North Cape route would be the Soviet Air Force's northern entry to western Europe, and to the United Kingdom. Consequently, Norwegian radar stations and interceptors are fully integrated in peacetime into the NATO command chain. The radar stations, as in the United Kingdom, are controlled by Operations Centres which exchange their air picture with the UK air defence units on a daily basis. This was the origin of the information which enabled the timely scramble of the 23 Squadron F3 and accompanying tanker in November 1989 which was described in Chapter 4. Regular joint exercises are held and Norwegian crew members and ground specialists participate in the NATO AWACs squadron. In wartime, aircraft from the E3 squadron at Geilenkirchen would deploy northwards to Orland Air Force Base in southern Norway.

A similar relationship exists between 11 Group and the Danish Air Defence system. For nearly 40 years daily exchange of information has taken place ensuring that the United Kingdom is kept aware of likely threats emanating from the Baltic. In war United Kingdom air defence operations would be mounted, with tanker support, close to the Jutland peninsula to protect the Danish 'back door' and provide extended, forward air defence to the United Kingdom itself. Like their Norwegian colleagues, Danish F16s regularly conduct joint exercises with RAF Tornadoes and Phantoms.

There is a further, unique connection

F16 of the Royal Norwegian Air Force *(RNAF)*

Royal Danish Air Force RF35 Draken *(RDAF)*

F16s of the Royal Belgian Air Force *(RBAF)*

between the two air defences. Some 300 miles north of the United Kingdom lies the Danish territory of the Faeroe Islands. Since 1963, a NATO early warning station has been operating on the island of Streymoy, built and manned by Denmark but under the operational control of the RAF Sector Operations Centre at Buchan as a fully integrated component of the United Kingdom Air Defence Ground Environment. Consequently, Danish controllers handle QRA Tornadoes and supporting tankers, and indeed any other RAF aircraft in

exactly the same way as Saxa Vord, Bishops Court or any other 11 Group CRP or CRC. There may be a different kind of secret on the Faeroes, because several of the Danish operations staff have volunteered to stay there for many years of duty. Major Freddy Hansen, a Royal Danish Air Force officer on the staff of HQUKAIR at High Wycombe, offered a clue: 'There is nothing like touring the Faeroes. Once you have shaken off the burdens of your work-a-day life and are able to see things once again as they really are, you will be at peace with yourself and the world'. Hopefully, the Buchan-Faeroes connection will remain a practical but superfluous guarantor of the sentiment.

Further south, in addition to alliance co-operation with the Royal Belgian Air Force, there is close RAF association with the main Belgian fighter base at Beauvechain. At the time of the German invasion of Belgium in May 1940, the second Belgian Air Regiment was equipped with 15 Hurricanes and 15 Gloster Gladiators. Within two days all 30 aircraft had been either destroyed or damaged and Beauvechain fell into Luftwaffe hands. Several of the surviving pilots made their way by various means across the Channel to join the RAF. In 1990, the two F16 squadrons at Beauvechain are numbers 349 and 350, but both squadrons have Royal Air Force crests, bearing the legend '349/350 (Belgian) Squadron, Royal Air Force'. Both were formed after the Battle of Britain in 1942 to give a corporate identity to the many young Belgians who wished to carry on the war against their country's invaders by fighting in the RAF.

Perhaps the closest of all the daily relationships between the 11 Group units and members of the Alliance is that with the United States Air Force. It dates back more than 70 years to a time when young United States Army Air Corps officers were strongly influenced by the leaders of the infant Royal Air Force to strive for their own independent service. The close cooperation of the Second World War years was soon extended to the post-war Alliance and the two air forces have collaborated at all levels since then. In 1990 there is regular contact between 11 Group aircraft and F15s from the USAF 28th Air Division detachment at Keflavik in Iceland. E3 AWACs aircraft are also detached to Keflavik from their home base with No 552 Wing at Tinker AFB in Oklahoma and the Buchan Sector maintains continuous communications with them in covering Britain's own northern flank.

In sum, the air defence of the British Isles in 1990 actually begins at the North Cape of Norway, extends down through central Europe and now also has a southern flank set of allies in France, Spain and Portugal. There are those who might recall that we had allies in 1939 also, but that by June 1940 we stood alone. There are in fact many differences, not least in the extent of close peacetime cooperation which has produced effective common procedures and a strong sense of mutual interdependence. There is also the hope that whereas 1940 was the beginning of dark days, 1990 offers hope of relaxation of political and military tensions not known since 1945.

In the last resort, however, the integrity of British airspace and the protection of the country below it, is the responsibility of the Royal Air Force, just as it was in 1940. The legacy of skies free from hostile intruders was bequeathed at great cost. Fifty years later, a new generation of young men and women have, by their constant preparedness, professional competence and unlimited commitment in the air and on the ground proved their fitness to inherit it.

Entente Cordiale: VC10K of No 101 Squadron with French Air Force Jaguar, Super Etendard and Mirage 2000 (Colonel Grosdemouche FAF)

EPILOGUE

O N 30 AUGUST 1940, the first German attacks were made shortly after dawn. Later in the morning, at half hourly intervals, three more waves of several hundred fighters and bombers. Then, continuous attacks from 1330 until early evening, and finally after nightfall 130 more Heinkels and Dorniers striking Liverpool and smaller groups striking targets across the whole of central and southern England.

They were opposed by 22 fighter squadrons whose pilots flew 1,054 sorties. It was the heaviest, most concentrated fighting yet encountered by Fighter Command's pilots. It was the first day of the critical period of the battle which was, unknown at the time by the Royal Air Force high command, to be decided in just nine days time.

On that hot Friday morning readers of *The Times* saw a letter from Viscount Wakefield which was self-explanatory.

'The wonderful achievements of the Royal Air Force in these critical weeks of the second Great War of our time have naturally led to various suggestions being made as to the best way in which we can give expression to our gratitude. In the deepest sense, there is no way in which the heroism and sacrifices of our airmen can be assessed or our debt to them in any way liquidated.

As there is, nevertheless the desire to express the nation's thanks in tangible form, let it be devoted in part to some constructive aim, some cause that can be shown to be solely and entirely for the permanent benefit of all ranks and their dependants. I venture to submit as the most appropriate object for our generosity, The Royal Air Force

The birthplace of Air Chief Marshal Lord Dowding at Moffat, Scotland now being converted to a sheltered housing development with funds raised in a joint appeal by the Royal Air Forces Association and The Royal Air Force Benevolent Fund *(RAF Benevolent Fund)*

Benevolent Fund, which exactly fulfils these conditions.

The Fund, founded in 1919 by Viscount Trenchard, in addition to assisting airmen in various circumstances of special need and difficulty, undertakes the education of children of Royal Air Force parentage and helps to establish them in careers that their fathers would be proud for them to follow.

Up to now, the funds of the Royal Air Force Benevolent Fund have been raised without any public appeal, largely by contributions from members of the Royal Air Force. It is only too sadly obvious that in the near future there must be heavy calls upon the Fund to an extent not at present calculable. With the gallant heroism of officers and men of the Royal Air Force before us day by day, I am confident that as a tribute to their ceaseless fight for the cause of freedom, many will wish to support their cause.'

Six years later, on Battle of Britain Sunday 1951, Sir Winston Churchill made a special radio appeal on behalf of the Benevolent Fund.

'Never in the field of human conflict was so much owed by so many to so few.' With those words in 1940 – our darkest and yet our finest hour – I reported to the House of Commons on the progress of the Battle of Britain, whose eleventh anniversary we now celebrate. I repeat my words tonight with pride and gratitude. They spring from our hearts as keenly at this moment as on the day I uttered them. Time dims our memories of many events which, while they are happening, seem tremendous. But the fame of the pilots – a thin blue line – indeed who broke the aerial might of the enemy and saved their native land shines ever more brightly. Our debt is now not only to 'The Few'. As the Royal Air Force grew larger and larger and the hard years of war unrolled, many thousands of their comrades died so that our island might live, free and inviolate. By 1945, alas, as our casualty lists told the tale. 'The Few' had become 'The Many'. Had it not been for those young men whose daring devotion cast a glittering shield between us and the foe, we should none of us be sitting at rest in our homes this Sunday evening, as members of an unconquered – and, as we believe, unconquerable – Nation. Let us welcome this chance to pay a small measure of the debt we owe to the paladins of the Royal Air Force. And I will tell you one thing we can do, and do now. I am appealing to you tonight on behalf of the Royal Air Force Benevolent Fund. This Fund exists solely to help members of the Royal Air Force – men and women – in time of need, and their families or dependants when they are in trouble . . . . The money which has been spent by the Royal Air Force Benevolent Fund has gone beyond the Fund's ordinary income . . . . A renewed effort must be made if the future is not to be overclouded . . . . It is our duty now to make sure that the Fund will be able to go on helping, and will not fail as the survivors of the war grow old and feeble. Only thus can the Fund maintain its claim and reputation that no genuine case of distress is ever turned away.

The Royal Air Force Benevolent Fund is part of the conscience of the British nation. A nation without a conscience is a nation without a soul. A nation without a soul is a nation that cannot live.'

By the end of the Second World War the 'many' servicemen and women who served in the Royal Air Force totalled one and three quarter million. Many are now reaching an age when they are increasingly likely to need the Fund's assistance. In 1988 15,880 beneficiaries received £8,641,262. The RAF Benevolent Fund could face this increasing demand upon its resources by imposing limits on the number of those to be helped, or ceilings on the individual amounts to be awarded. Either course would contradict the principles which have been applied throughout the Fund's existence: to establish the exact nature of the individual difficulty, and then respond to it in

Below left: Mk IIc Hurricane carrying the code GN–A, representing the aircraft flown by Flight Lieutenant James Nicholson of No 249 Squadron when he won his Victoria Cross in August 1940, has its cockpit canopy jettison mechanism checked by Corporal Peter Jeffrey *(Author)*
Below: Mark Vb Spitfire AB 910, presented to the Battle of Britain Memorial Flight by the American Research Foundation has its instrument panel wiring checked by Corporal Steve Ball in preparation for the 1990 display season *(Author)*

full. Consequently, in 1990 the RAF Benevolent Fund is commemorating the sacrifices of all those men and women who took part in the epic Battle of Britain and the many other air operations of the Second World War by an appeal to raise an additional £20 million, an appeal known as 'Reach for the Sky'.

One RAF Unit links the aircraft of 1940, the aircrew and groundcrew of 1990, and the remembrance appeal: the Battle of Britain Memorial Flight at RAF Coningsby. The Flight of Spitfires, Hurricanes and Lancaster was formed at Biggin Hill in July 1957 to commemorate the Service's major Battle Honour and to serve as a reminder of the vital role played by the Royal Air Force in the defence of the country. Among the Spitfires and Hurricanes flown by the Flight is P7350, a Mk IIa Spitfire which was built at Castle Bromwich in 1940 and entered service with 266 Squadron in August at Tangmere.

The senior fighter pilot in the Flight is Wing Commander David Moss, otherwise employed as OC Operations Wing at Coningsby with over 3,000 flying hours on Lightnings, Phantoms and Tornadoes. He heads a small num-

ber of fighter pilots, all current on modern front line fast jets, who have enthusiastically grasped an opportunity to devote many weekends to demonstrating the excellence and appeal of the Hurricane and Spitfire alongside the Flight's representative for Bomber Command, Lancaster P4 474, City of Lincoln.

The Inheritance

The skies above Britain in 1990 are free from the sound of gunfire. Since 1945, behind strong defences, western Europe has enjoyed unprecedented prosperity and the longest period of peace the continent has known. There are hopeful signs that, despite remaining sources of instability in eastern Europe, the tensions created by political and military confrontation from the Soviet Union and her allies are fast disappearing. If so, the state of readiness demanded of the Royal Air Force, and especially from the men and women of 11 Group, may come to be relaxed. The world however will remain unpredictable. In 1919 there were hopes of universal peace, in 1945 celebrations and great optimism. In 1957, for different reasons, it was believed that Britain would not be threatened again by manned aircraft. Only future uncertainty is certain.

The legacy of peaceful skies, inherited by the men and women of 11 Group and protected so comprehensively with so much dedication over so many years should not be lightly cast away. Long before the first Rolls-Royce Merlin engine was heard over England, Benjamin Franklin commented: 'One sword keeps another in its scabbard.' Today he would see that the sacrifices of 1940 had not been in vain; that lessons had been learned and remembered; that were they ever to be called upon in anger, there is skill, bravery and loyalty in today's aircrew and ground crew worthy of their predecessors. He would see it, and he would approve.

A CONTRAST IN TYPES
THE AIRCRAFT OF 1940 AND 1990

The Aircraft in 1940

In 1940, Fighter Command deployed four types of fighters: the Hawker Hurricane Mark I, the Supermarine Spitfire Mark 1A, the Bristol Blenheim Mark IF and the Boulton Paul Defiant I.

The Hurricane

1715 Hurricanes bore the brunt of the Battle of Britain. Designed by Sydney Camm, it was powered by a single 1,030 h.p. Rolls-Royce Merlin III 12 cylinder liquid cooled engine. It had a wing span of 40 feet and was 31 feet 4 inches long. It had a maximum speed of 328 m.p.h. at 20,000 feet and a ceiling of 34,200 feet. Its maximum range was 500 miles. It was inferior to the Spitfire in speed and climb but was highly manoeuvrable and could take a great deal of battle damage. It is believed that its pilots accounted for more than three-quarters of all Luftwaffe combat casualties between July and October, with its 8 .303 inches calibre Browning machine guns.

The Spitfire

The Spitfire was designed by R J Mitchell who tragically did not live to see the outstanding contribution of his aircraft to the RAF in the Second World War. By 19 July, squadrons were equipped with the Mark 1A. It was slightly smaller than the Hurricane: 36 feet 11 inches wing span and 29 feet 11 inches long, and the direct descendant of the S6B seaplanes which had won the Schneider Trophy outright for Britain in 1931. It had a maximum speed of 362 m.p.h., a ceiling of 31,900 feet and a range of 400 miles. It was very fast, highly manoeuvrable, light on the controls and capable of rapid acceleration. As a result, it posed a severe threat to the ME 109 in one-on-one combat. During the Battle, most Spitfires were powered by the Merlin III engine and armed, like the Hurricane, with 8 .303 machine guns. But whereas the Hurricane was steadily removed from front line operations as the war progressed, the Spitfire was repeatedly modified and remained in service for several years after 1945. It was always a pilot's aeroplane and has now passed into national legend.

The Blenheim

The Bristol Blenheim fighter was developed from an original design by Frank Barnwell and began service life as a bomber. Pressed into service as a day fighter in 1939 it suffered heavy losses, but proved an excellent test bed for the infant night fighter force before being replaced by the specialist Beaufighter later in the war. It had a 54 feet wing span and was 39 feet 9 inches long. Powered by twin 840 h.p. Bristol Mercury VIII engines it had a maximum speed of 285 m.p.h. at 15,000 feet, a range of 1,125 miles and a ceiling of 27,280 feet. It was armed with 5 .303 Browning and one .303 Vickers machine guns.

The Defiant

The Boulton Paul Defiant was originally designed to mount defensive patrols against relatively slow bombers of an earlier generation, but in the critical days of 1940, it was pressed into service as an interceptor. It was powered by the same Merlin engine as the Hurricane and Spitfire but its aerodynamic shape and weight restricted its speed to 300 m.p.h., with a range of 465 miles and a service ceiling of 30.350 feet. At first, its four rearward facing .303 Browning guns in an electrically operated turret were effective, but it had neither speed nor manoeuvrability to survive in a dogfight and its squadrons suffered terrible casualties at the hands of the ME 109, especially as it was very difficult for the rear gunner to get out of his turret in a hurry. By 1 August, the two Defiant squadrons, Nos 141 and 264, had been withdrawn from the front line well out of Messerschmitt reach.

The Aircraft in 1990

In 1990, seven of the nine fighter squadrons of 11 Group are equipped with the Panavia Tornado F3, two with the McDonnell-Douglas F4 Phantom, and wartime reinforcement would come from the British Aerospace Hawks of the TWUs at Chivenor and Brawdy.